TABLE OF CONTENTS

OBSTACLES TO PROTECTING THE AMAZON

LIST OF ILLUSTRATIONS

PAGE

SECURITY OF BRAZILIAN AMAZON AREA

INTRODUCTION

The Brazilian Amazon is, undeniably, an area of great geopolitical and ecological importance. The Amazon is characterized by large territorial expanse, demographic emptiness, long borders, abundant natural resources (particularly water and mineral resources), socio-economic complications, and considerable international interest in the region. Altogether, these factors give the region its particular complexity as an international geopolitical issue.

The Brazilian Amazon's geopolitical importance demands preservation of the natural environment and development of the area as part of the larger Amazon region. Geographically, the Amazon is a huge basin that drains an area of 7,300,000 square kilometers in the northern part of the South American continent. It encompasses territory in seven countries besides Brazil: Guyana, Suriname, French Guiana, Venezuela, Colombia, Peru, and Ecuador (Figure 1).

In 1978, Brazil took the initiative to bring eight neighboring countries into the Treaty of Amazonian Cooperation, or the Pan Amazonic Treaty. The 28 articles included the following emphases:

1. Development of the region was the exclusive competence of these countries,

2. Preservation of natural resources was also part of their national sovereignty,

FIGURE 1

3. The countries agreed to cooperate to achieve these two objectives,

4. Harmony between development and ecological protection should be achieved, and

5. The countries would cooperate on health care, river navigation, road building, scientific research, conservation, and tourism.

International greed and attempts to interfere in the Brazilian Amazon area, have been amply reported in the press. Examples of these include the following:

1. In 1967/1968, the Hudson Institute proposed a project conceived by the futurist Herman Khan, known as the "Great Amazon Lakes", that would have flooded an area fifteen times bigger than all the other proposed projects for this region combined.[1] Brazil rejected the idea,

2. The Christian Church World Council, since 1981, has emphasized the following to their missionaries in the Amazon: "The entire Amazon, a large portion of which is enclosed by Brazil, but also includes territories of Venezuela, Colombia and Peru, is considered by us a patrimony of humanity. Ownership of this vast area by the mentioned countries is merely circumstantial... The natives who live there are considered to be "inherited" by humanity, and do not belong to the countries who are supposed to be their owners...",[2]

3

3. Foreign organizations, such as "Survival International" - based in London, "Cultural Survival" and "Gaia Foundation" - based in the United States - et al., attempt to create multinationally-supervised indian reservations,[3]

4. Tin-exporting countries have interfered politically to maintain the international prices of that metal, in order to block Brazilian production,[4]

5. Two United States groups, "The Environmental Defense Fund" and "The National Wildlife Federation", have pressured the Inter American Development Bank (IDB) to provide protection for the rain forest and the Indians. In December 1987, the bank suspended the $58.5 million project loan because Brazil's federal government "had failed to create institutions to prevent unchecked devastation of the forest and the overruning of Indian lands",[5]

6. European parliamentarians worked, in 1989, through the European Economic Community (EEC) to try to interrupt the Carajás Project in the southern area of Pará State (eastern Amazon), in order to keep it from exporting iron ore to many countries in the world,[6]

7. In 1989, a subsidiary of Japan's Mitsubishi Corporation offered to buy Brazil's $115 billion foreign debt in exchange for mining rights over Amazon gold fields.

At that time, Brazil's President José Sarney said that "Brazil's sovereignty cannot be swapped for anything"[7],

8. President George Bush, under the aegis of environmentalism, prevent Japan from granting the financing for construction of a road linking Brazil and Peru - the first road from the Pacific into Amazonia. He claimed that the road would cause irreparable damage to the Amazon rain forest.[8] Also, American Senator Albert Gore called the road "a catastrophe waiting to happen". He proposed legislation to protect the Amazon by pressuring lenders to fund only ecologically sound development,[9]

9. In early 1989, American Senators Albert Gore and John Chafee visited the Amazon and afterwards said: "The devastation is just unbelievable".[10] At the same time, American Senator Robert Kasten told about the imperative of protecting "our Amazon", that one nation often does have a legitimate interest in the environmental practices of another,[11]

10. Mr. Michel Rocard, French Prime Minister, has suggested forgiveness of Brazil's external debt for a guarantee of the forest's preservation.[12] This proposal was endorsed by American Senators John Heinz and Timothy Wirth who stated to the *Christian Science Monitor* that "Brazil is burdened by an overwelming foreign debt. In a debt-forest swamp pro.ram, Brazil could exchange

conservation of a set piece of forest for forgiveness of a certain amount of debt - an arragement that benefits all of us environmentally and Brazil economically, as well",[13]

11. Thomas Lovejoy, a tropical ecologist and assistant secretary for external affairs at the Smithsonian Institution, in 1989, was also a leading proponent of the concept of "debt-for-nature swaps",[14]

12. The U.N. environmental commission chaired by Norway's Labor Party Prime Minister Gro Harlem Brundtland observed, "the traditional forms of national sovereignty are increasingly challenged by the realities of ecological and economic interdependence",[15]

13. Mr. Noel Brown, The United Nations Environment Program (UNEP) chairman has stated: "I think the environment issue will rule the relations between countries and people. It will also re-examine the matter of territorial sovereignty",[16]

14. On October 16, 1990, In Paris, "People Permanent Tribunal" - an entity subordinated to "The Internatinal League for Rights and Libertation of People", - which has a consultant *status* in the United Nation - put Brazil in a "prisoner's dock" and considered it "guilty" for adopting a predatory economic model for Amazonia and for "acts that killed a great number of

Yanomami Indians and other indigenous groups". "The court's president" was the Belgian professor François Rigaux, and among the "members of the jury" were the French First Lady, Danielle Miterrand, and the writer Adolfo Perez Esquivel - winner of the Nobel Peace Prize,[17]

15. French President François Mitterrand championed a variety of social colonialist ideas, which he defended at the 1989 Conference on Ecology at The Hague. He urged, unsuccessfully, the formation of a supranational body to evaluate the behavior of governments on environmental matters,[18]

16. In 1990, the American ecology entity Rainforest Action Network - based in San Francisco - started a campaign against the World Bank and the International Monetary Fund for loaning money to Brazil which "despises the environment's security". In the New York Times, this entity asked to readers to lobby their congressmen in order to block funds for those international financial institutions[19] and,

17. In 1991 the German chancellor, Helmut Kohl, said that "the countries constituting the so-called Group of Seven need to reach an agreement with the Brazilian government so that rules for the administration of the Amazon can be established".[20]

Such statements, combined with the widely-held view that the Amazon forest is the only great rain forest in the world, suggest that international designs on the Amazon could directly affect Brazilian sovereignty (Figure 2).[21]

Given the vastness of the Amazon area, the preceding remarks, and the complexities of the various issues involved, analysis of this matter must not be restricted to the tactical or even operational levels, but to the strategic one. This is necessary because Brazilian Military Manuals distinguish between these terms, and give the concept of security a strategic sense of *state/condition*, which must be achieved and maintained.

This paper:

o states Brazil's interests and objectives in Amazonia.

o identifies current threats to the Brazilian Amazon,

o identifies the real motivations and origins of those threats, and

o recommends measures to overcome those threats.

AMAZON RAIN FOREST

RAIN FOREST

FIGURE 2

ANALYSIS OF THE AREA

"The Amazon is the final page of Genesis, yet to be
written with such sharpness and emotion that it seems
to throb with fever. It is a thousand-year war against
the unknown, whose victory will come after incalculable
labors, in a future most remote, when the veritable
veils of that marvelous place are torn away. Meanwhile,
it is the maiden land, the young land, the land that
is, the land still growing".[22]

GEOPOLITICAL ASPECTS

This examination of the Amazon issue must initially define
and demarcate the area, henceforth referred to as "Legal Amazon",
because publications have referred to the area in many different
ways.

Encompassing the drainage basins of the Amazon, Tocantins,
and Araguaia rivers, the region covers 4,375,000 square miles in
the northern part of South America. The area, covered mainly by a
humid tropical forest called "Hylea" by Humboldt, includes parts
of the countries of Bolivia, Peru, Ecuador, Colombia, Venezuela,
Guyana, Suriname, French Guiana, and Brazil (Figure 3).

Over 60% of the area, about 3,125,000 square miles is
Brazilian territory. This accounts for 60% of the total land area
of Brazil, including parts of the states of Acre, Amazonas,
Roraima, Pará, Amapá, Mato Grosso, Tocantins and the western
region of Maranhão (Figure 4).

To better visualize the vastness of this expanse, consider
that it could hold simultaneously within its boundaries the
following European countries: Portugal, Spain, Ireland, Great

FIGURE 3

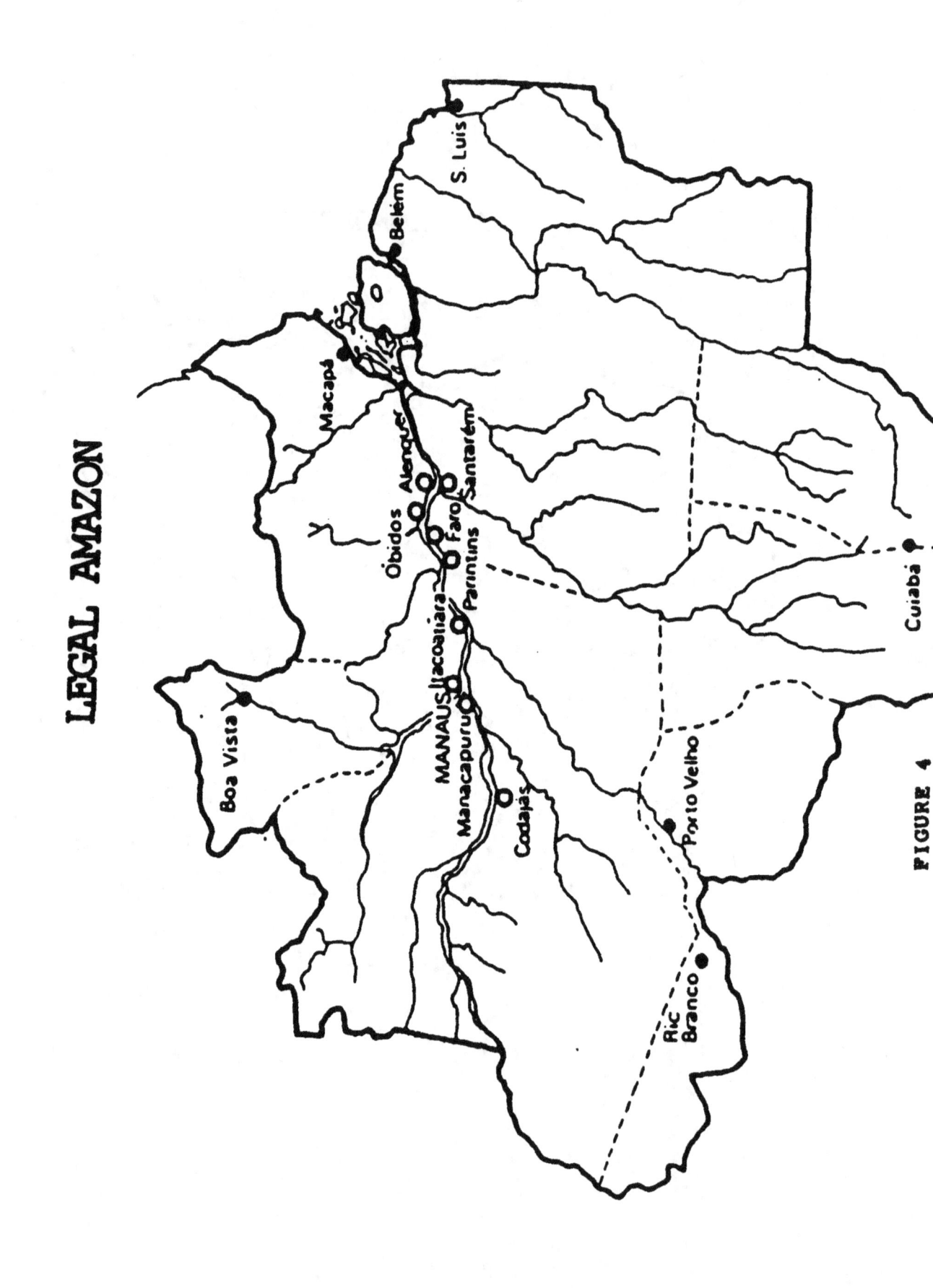

LEGAL AMAZON

FIGURE 4

Britain, Belgium, The Netherlands, Germany, Switzerland, Italy, Austria, Hungary, Czechoslovakia, Yugoslavia, and Albania (Figure 5).

Professor Samuel Benchimol of the Amazon State University puts it clearly, as follows: "On a picture of the planet Earth taken from Mars, the enormous Amazonian region could be described in the following way:

- . 1/20 of the earth's land surface;
- . 4/10 of South America;
- . 3/5 of Brazil;
- . 1/5 of the world's available drinking water ,and
- . 1/3 of the world latiofoliate forest reserves".[23]

In terms of geographic boundaries, part of Brazil's territory shares frontiers with French Guiana, Suriname, Guyana, Venezuela, Colombia, Peru and Bolivia. This is a border of 6,000 miles, or over 60% of Brazil's land frontiers.

The Brazilian Amazon's coastline measures 1,125 miles, stretching from Cape Orange in Amapá State, to São Luis in the state of Maranhão.

SOCIOPSYCHOLOGICAL ASPECTS

Climate

The Amazon's climate is typically equatorial, homogenous throughout the year, with high mean temperatures and rainfall of 78°F and 80 inches, respectively.[24]

LEGAL AMAZON - COMPARISON

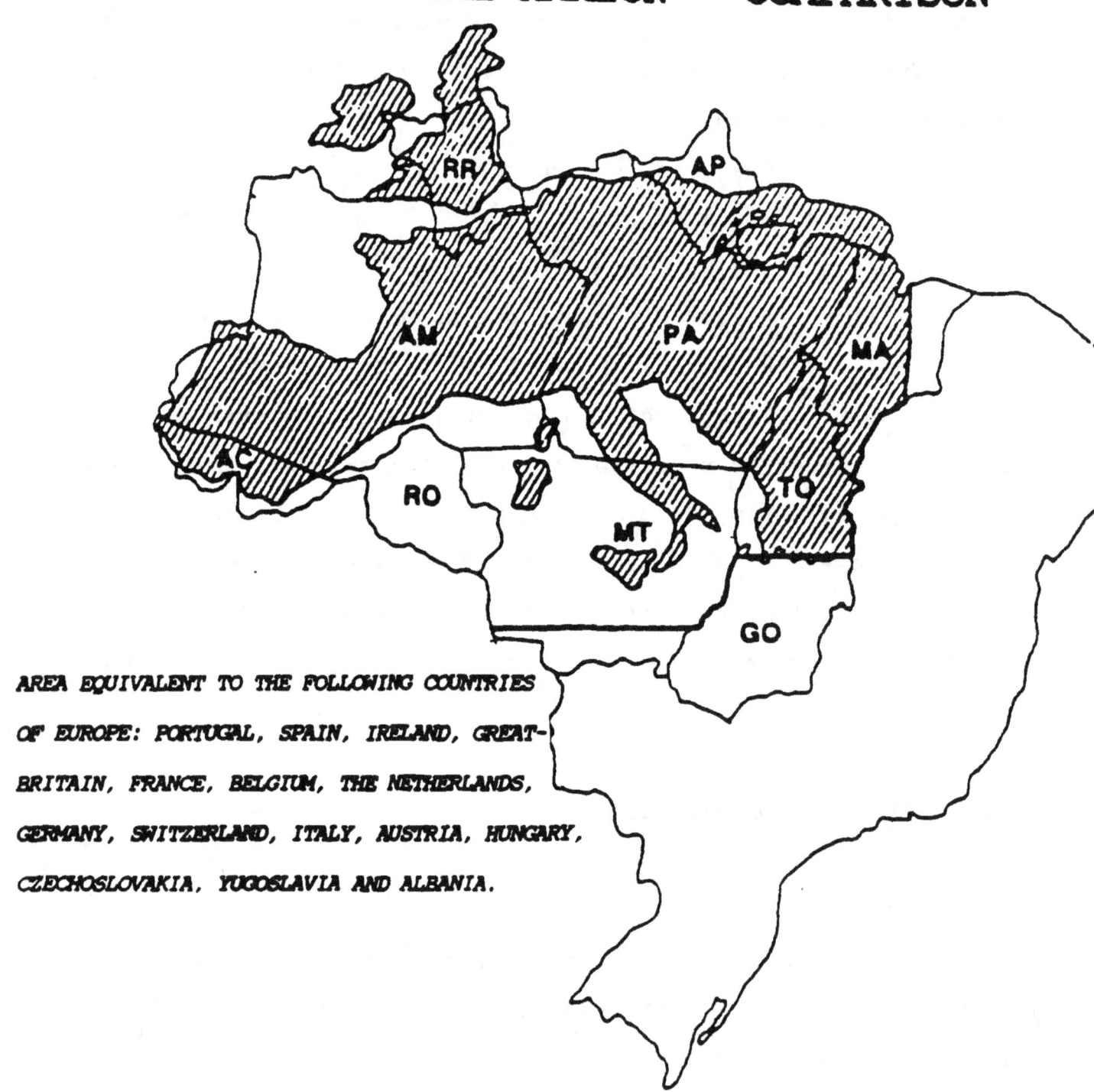

AREA EQUIVALENT TO THE FOLLOWING COUNTRIES OF EUROPE: PORTUGAL, SPAIN, IRELAND, GREAT-BRITAIN, FRANCE, BELGIUM, THE NETHERLANDS, GERMANY, SWITZERLAND, ITALY, AUSTRIA, HUNGARY, CZECHOSLOVAKIA, YUGOSLAVIA AND ALBANIA.

FIGURE 5

14

There is, however, a short dry season of two to four months, particularly along a wide stretch joining Roraima to Central Brazil. The temperatures in that area are not very high in themselves, but the humid air is produces discomfort that makes life so much harder in that area.

Vegetation

The region's vegetation is very diverse. Understandably, in such an enormous expanse, one finds great diversity of land and aquatic ecosystems integrated in a wide variety of scenic settings.

More than half of this area is covered by humid equatorial and tropical forests, presently the focus of much speculation that provided much of the stimulus for this paper.

Contrary to what some would have us believe, not all the Amazon area is covered by tropical forest. Extensive prairies and areas of open pasture with patches of stunted vegetation can be found in the states of Roraima, Amapá, Tocantins, and Pará.[25]

Topography

The region's relief is formed basically by a huge sedimentary basin, bordered by the crystalline shields of the Massif of Guyana and the Massif of Brazil. In the east-west direction, the basin stretches from the Atlantic Ocean to the Andes.

Brazil's highest elevation is at "Misty Peak", with an elevation of 9,042 feet, in the Massif of Guyana, in Roraima state.

Hydrography

The region has a rich fluvial system, with some 15,500 miles of navigable rivers, and including the continent's main rivers. The Amazon river, the greatest of these, is fed by more than 1,000 tributaries and meanders for 4,000 miles, a length second only to the Nile's 4,100 miles. Some 2,500 of these miles are within Brazilian territory. The Amazon's average width is 4 miles; even 1,000 miles upriver it is often impossible to see from one side of the Amazon to the other. During the floods, it overflows its banks an average of about 32 miles and reaches, at its mouth, a width of 250 miles.[26] It has a depth of between 65 feet and 97 feet, and large-tonnage boats can navigate up to Manaus 800 miles upstream without difficulty, even during the low water periods. The size and capacity of the Amazon are essential for the economy and for maintaining the regional ecologic balance, as well as for transportation.

SOCIAL ASPECTS

Population

The Amazon population is estimated at 16.5 million (11% of the Brazilian population), of which 60% are urban dwellers. Its demographic density is low: about three inhabitants per square kilometer.[27] The rural areas are inhabited by settled farming populations, squatters in the agricultural frontier, riverine communities, gold-miners, rubber tappers, and indians. Today, internal migration, more than reproductive growth, accounts for most of the Amazon's population increase.

Education and Culture

Education and culture vary greatly between the urban and the rural areas. In the former, the government's educational system proceeds normally, thus permitting the integration of those populations into present-day Brazilian culture. In this regard, land communications play a fundamental role. In the capitals of the region's bigger states, access to higher education (universities) is straightforward.

In the remote areas, far from the urban centers, the educational process breaks down somewhat, leading to underdevelopment of rural areas compared to the median social and cultural standards of the Brazilian people.

The Brazilian Army plays a valuable role in the remote areas of the Amazonian territory, by providing basic education to the indigenous people in schools operated by the militaries.

Health and Nutrition

In isolated areas, both medical assistance and sanitary conditions are deficient and the population's food consists basically of fish and the products of subsistence agriculture.

There is a very high level of tropical diseases, with an equally high death rate among young children. In the urban areas, patients can be attended to by the official health services which, nonetheless, are still inadequate for the real needs of certain areas.

Employment, Welfare and Social Services

In the area of employment, welfare, and social services, too, the analysis must consider differences between urban and rural areas. In the latter, productive activities are mainly concentrated in agriculture, cattle-ranching, forestry, exploitation of vegetable resources, hunting and fishing. In the urban areas, on the other hand, there is a tendency toward industrialization and excessive concentration of urban population, with the usual attendant risks of an oversupply of labor and a tendency toward underemployment, poorly paid jobs, and disregard for labor laws due to an emerging underground economy. Welfare and social services are also insufficient to satisfy the needs of the population.

ECONOMIC ASPECTS

A large portion of the population relies on subsistence agriculture. Manaus is the main industrial center, where, because of its Free Trade Zone, several electronics industries have been established. The road system, although expanding, is still inadequate for the needs of the region, and the region's rivers continue to be the most used internal means of communication.

The mineral wealth of the Brazilian Amazon has been estimated at $30 trillion, with deposits of gold, tin, iron, copper, bauxite, uranium, potassium, rare earths, niobium, sulphur, manganese, diamonds and other precious stones, and possibly petroleum.[28] New mineral deposits are still being discovered (Figure 6).

Economic projects in the Amazon began in the 1920s and '30s, when Henry Ford tried twice to carve rubber empires out of the rain forest. But when the protective canopy was cut down, the rubber trees withered under the assault of the sun, rain and pests. In 1967 Daniel Ludwig, an American billionaire, launched a rashly ambitious project to clear 2.5 million acres of forest and plant gmelina trees for their timber. He believed that the imported species would not be susceptible to Brazil's pests. Ludwig was wrong, and as his trees died off, he bailed out of the project in 1982.[29]

The Brazilian government, meanwhile, came up with development schemes of its own. In the early 1970s the country built the Trans-Amazon Highway, a system of roads running west from the coastal city of Recife toward the Peruvian border. The idea was to prompt a land rush similar to that of the American West. To encourage settlers to brave the jungle, the government

NATURAL RESOURCES IN BRAZILIAN AMAZONIA

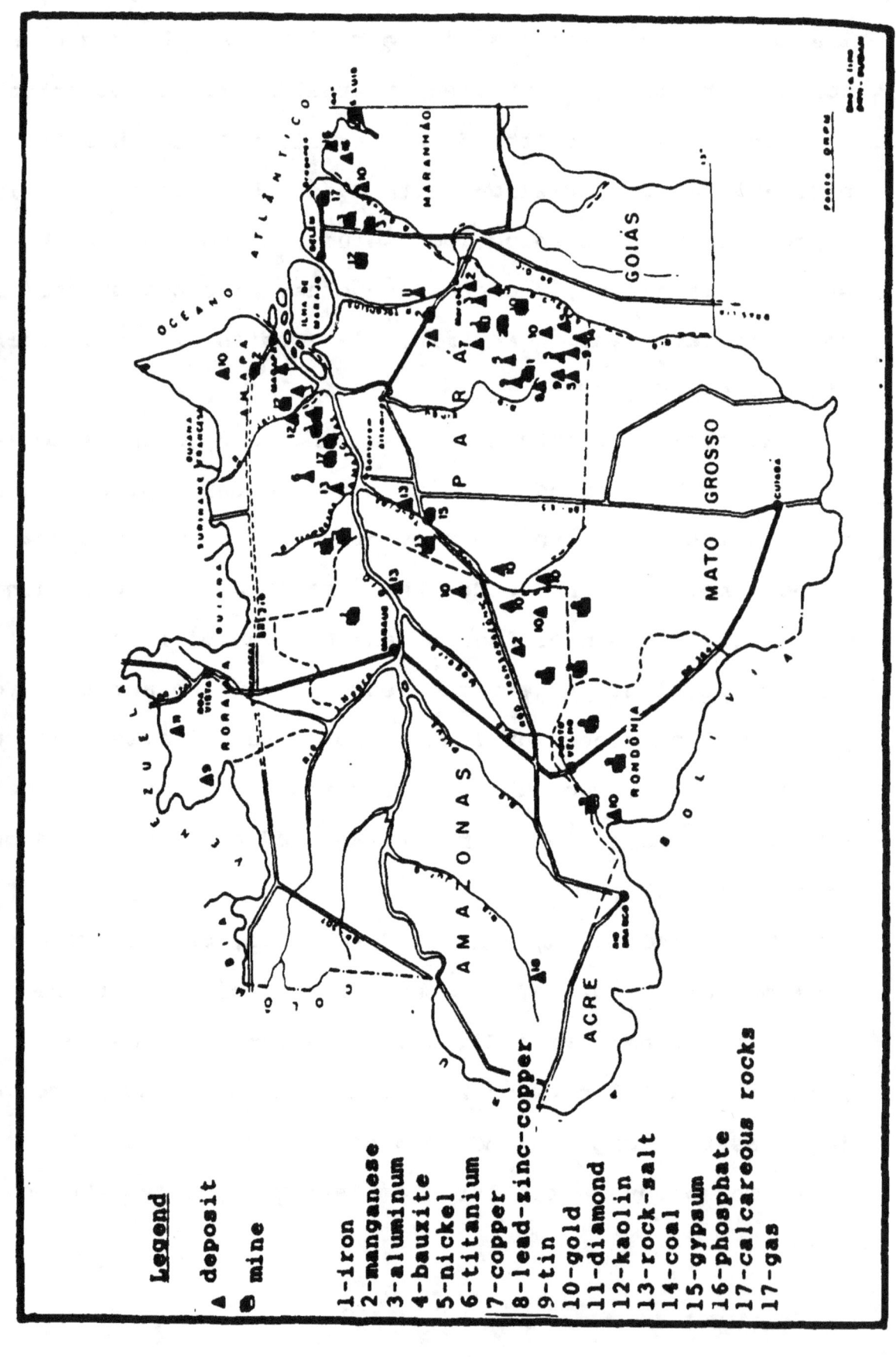

Legend

▲ deposit
⬟ mine

1—iron
2—manganese
3—aluminum
4—bauxite
5—nickel
6—titanium
7—copper
8—lead-zinc-copper
9—tin
10—gold
11—diamond
12—kaolin
13—rock-salt
14—coal
15—gypsum
16—phosphate
17—calcareous rocks
17—gas

FIGURE 6

offered transportation and other incentives. More than 8,000
families settled down along the Trans-Amazon Highway.

After implementing this project, Brazil continued to build
roads, dams (in particular Tucuruí hydroelectric power plant) and
settlements, often with funding and technical advice from the
World Bank, the European Community, and Japan. Two of the largest
projects are Great Carajás, a giant development program that
includes a major mining complex, and Polonoroeste, a highway and
settlement scheme.

The Great Carajás Project, costing $3.5 billion, covers
324,000 square miles in the eastern Amazon and seeks to exploit
Brazil's mineral deposits. Its main iron ore mine began
production in 1985; operations have had little impact on the
forest.[30]

In the other huge project, Polonoroeste, the government is
trying to develop the sprawling western state of Rondônia. The
program, backed by subsidies, and built around a highway through
the state called BR-364, was designed to relieve population
pressures in southern Brazil (Figure 7).

Finally, concerning fossil fuels, the Brazilian Oil Company
- PETROBRÁS - has confirmed discovery of an estimated 30 billion
cubic meters of recoverable dry natural gas (methane) in the
vicinity of the river Juruá, 470 miles southwest of Manaus.[31]

In 1986, PETROBRÁS discovered petroleum and natural gas with
a commercial potential in a paleozoic sedimentary basin along the
river Urucú, 400 miles southwest of Manaus. The basin may have an

21

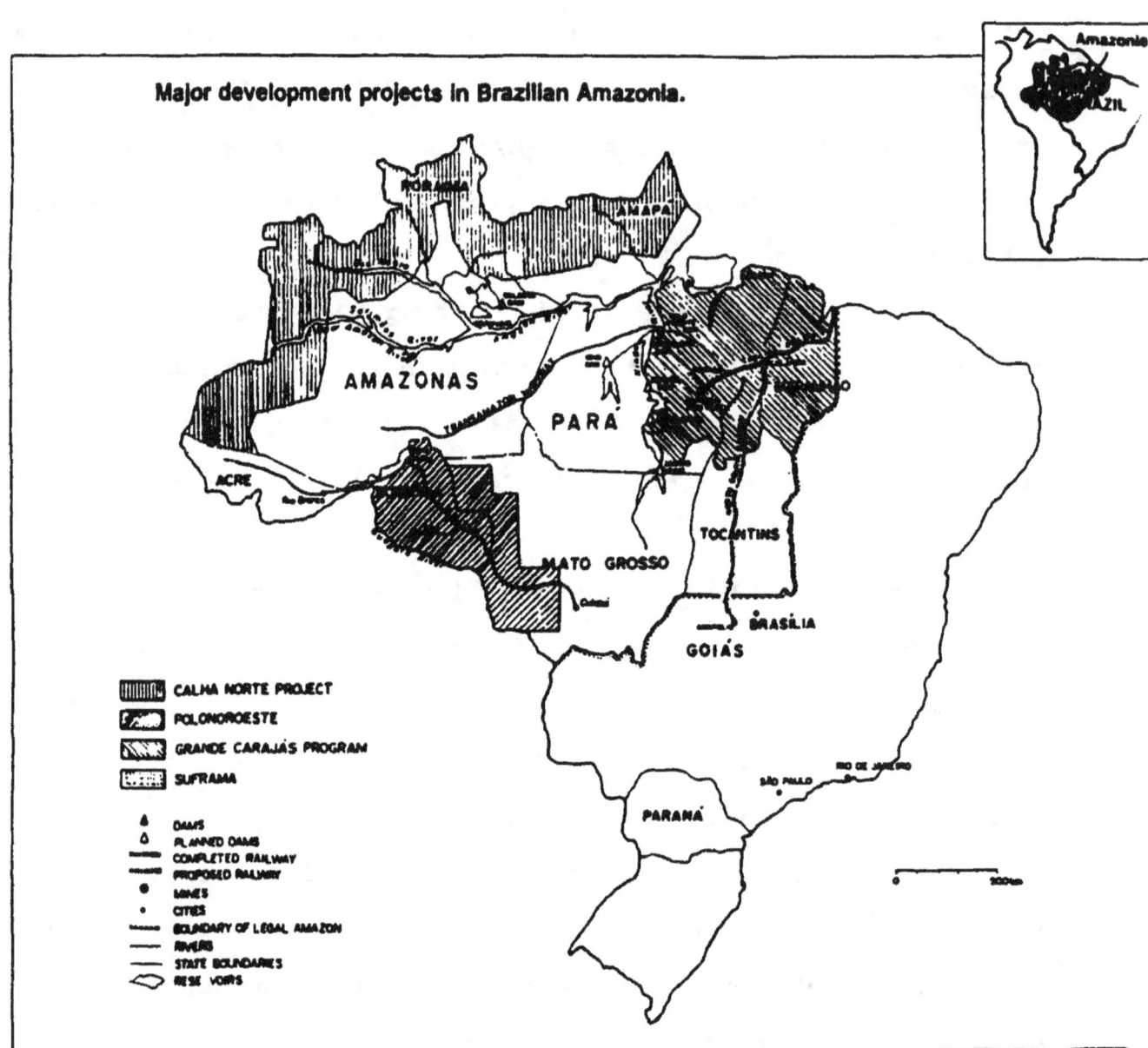

Major development projects in Brazilian Amazonia.

FIGURE 7

area as large as 60 square miles. The potential recoverable volumes are 20 million barrels of oil of excellent quality, with "oil in place" estimated at 110 million barrels, along with 15 million barrels of condensed gas and 20 billion cubic meters of rich gas. Commercial exploitation of the oil has already begun, with an actual daily production of 4,500 barrels through 10 wells.[32] Many areas of the Amazon remain to be explored.

CURRENT ROLE OF THE ARMED FORCES

Today, Brazil is geographically divided into military regions, each with its own military headquarters. In the Amazon region, the Army, Navy, and Air Force each have military headquarters.

During the whole republican era (i.e, since 1889) and especially in the last few years, the Brazilian Armed Forces, the Army in particular, have concentrated strongly on supporting the Federal Government's efforts to integrate the Amazon region with the rest of the country.

The mission of the Military Command of the Amazon can be summarized, as follows: providing internal and external security, and cooperating in the development of the areas furthest removed from the great population centers. This translates into the following tasks:

- establishment of settlements, which entails settling civilian populations around the most remote military units,

23

- education, in all frontier units, using state teachers or their own personnel; the norm is elementary, junior high, and high school,

- health, an item that stands out because, in several interior centers and in the border areas, only the Army is able to provide public health services (normally, care to Brazilian military personnel represents only 15 to 20% of care provided by the Brazilian military doctors -- the other 80 to 85% of the time they attend to indians, civilians and military personnel from bordering countries), and

- transportation routes, particularly through efforts of the 2nd Construction Engineering Group in building and maintaining roads throughout the Amazon region. This group can also carry out military missions and construction of infrastructure anywhere in the country.

Use of military units in the Amazon is beneficial because the skills of soldiers can be honed and expanded in far and inhospitable regions.

The Jungle Warfare Training Center ("CIGS"), created in March 1964 to instruct and train troops for operations in the Amazon region, deserves special mention. The CIGS is internationally known for its training standards as well as for advances in the doctrine and research fields. Delegations from many friendly countries have sought first-hand knowledge of what some consider the best jungle warfare training school anywhere.[33]

In its 27 years of existence, the CIGS has graduated 1,764 highly-specialized jungle experts, of which 144 are from friendly nations, including Argentina, Bolivia, Chile, Colombia, Ecuador, England, France, Guatemala, Guyana, Mexico, Panama, Paraguay, Peru, Portugal, Suriname and the USA.[34]

Most of the missions described above are the reponsability of the Brazilian Army. However, because of the area's extremely difficult terrain, the Army relies on support from the other forces.

The Brazilian Air Force (FAB), besides carrying out the normal duties expected of it in the area, supports the Army in transport and training with helicopters (Super Puma and UH-1H) and fixed-wing aircraft (Hercules, Buffalo, and Bandeirantes).

Similarly, the Brazilian Navy (MB), also provides transportation and training support to the Army, with river patrol boats, landing craft, and fast assault boats.

THE AMAZON CONQUEST

"The Amazon basin was a Spanish discovery, but a Portuguese conquest; on the other hand, the River Plate basin was a Portuguese discovery, but a Spanish conquest".[35]

Historical attempts to integrate the Amazon into the remainder of what is today Brazil include both the Portuguese-Brazilian conquest, and modern attempts to link the region to the

Brazilian heartland through a rail and road network (the so-called "Geopolitical Maneuver").

THE PORTUGUESE-BRAZILIAN CONQUEST

The Treaty of Tordesilhas[36] of 1494 divided the Western Hemisphere, from pole to pole, between Spain and Portugal along a vertical line that ran near the mouth of the Amazon river; but the Portuguese-Brazilians moved well westward of this line as early as the 16th century. In the south, *bandeirantes*[37] from the area which is today São Paulo penetrated into the interior on raids against the Jesuit missions in the Paraná basin or on expeditions to capture indigenous slaves or discover gold. In the north, Portuguese speakers ascended the Amazon river and its tributaries, and in the center the São Francisco river. Spanish speakers, in contrast, tended to settle in the highlands of northern and western South America, leaving the Amazonian lowlands unoccupied.

In 1616, Francisco Caldeira Castello Branco founded Belém do Pará, by building a fort. This was the beginning of the occupation of the Amazon, which was coveted in those days by the Dutch, French and British, who navigated in the lower Amazon river, explored the region, carried on trade with the natives, founded commercial posts, and built small forts.

Captain Pedro Teixeira, a great Portuguese soldier, became the most renowned explorer in the Amazon. He commanded a great expedition that set out in 1637 from Quito, Ecuador to explore the Amazon. Then followed the calm and organized occupation of the area by missionaries, soldiers, and explorers that guaranteed the Amazon. By the end of 17th century, bronze and iron cannons were defending Fort São José do Rio Negro, nowadays Manaus.

Portugal defended the Amazon territories so arduously conquered. It established, despite difficulties, posts that left no doubt about the borders of Brazil. During the 17th, 18th and 19th centuries, about 37 forts were founded in the Amazon[38] (Figure 8). The forts built during the 17th century had the mission of occupying the Amazon river mouth, defending it against the British, French and Dutch. In the 18th century, fortifications were established in the far west of the Amazon, defending the main avenues of approach to the Brazilian territory from the Spanish colonies.

The Treaty of Madrid (1750) and the Treaty of San Ildefonso (1777) recognized the *de facto* Portuguese occupation of the interior of the continent, though they left the precise borders vague. The principle of *uti possidetis*[39] underlay these treaties, which meant that sovereignty depended on actual occupation of the territory - in this case, by people whose sense of identity was Portuguese.

In the 19th century, a series of treaties with Peru in 1851, Venezuela in 1859, and Bolivia in 1867 provided the backdrop for the extraordinary territorial acquisitions of José Maria da Silva Paranhos Júnior, the Baron of Rio Branco.

HISTORIC FORTIFICATIONS IN AMAZON
(17ᵗʰ, 18ᵗʰ, and 19ᵗʰ Centuries)

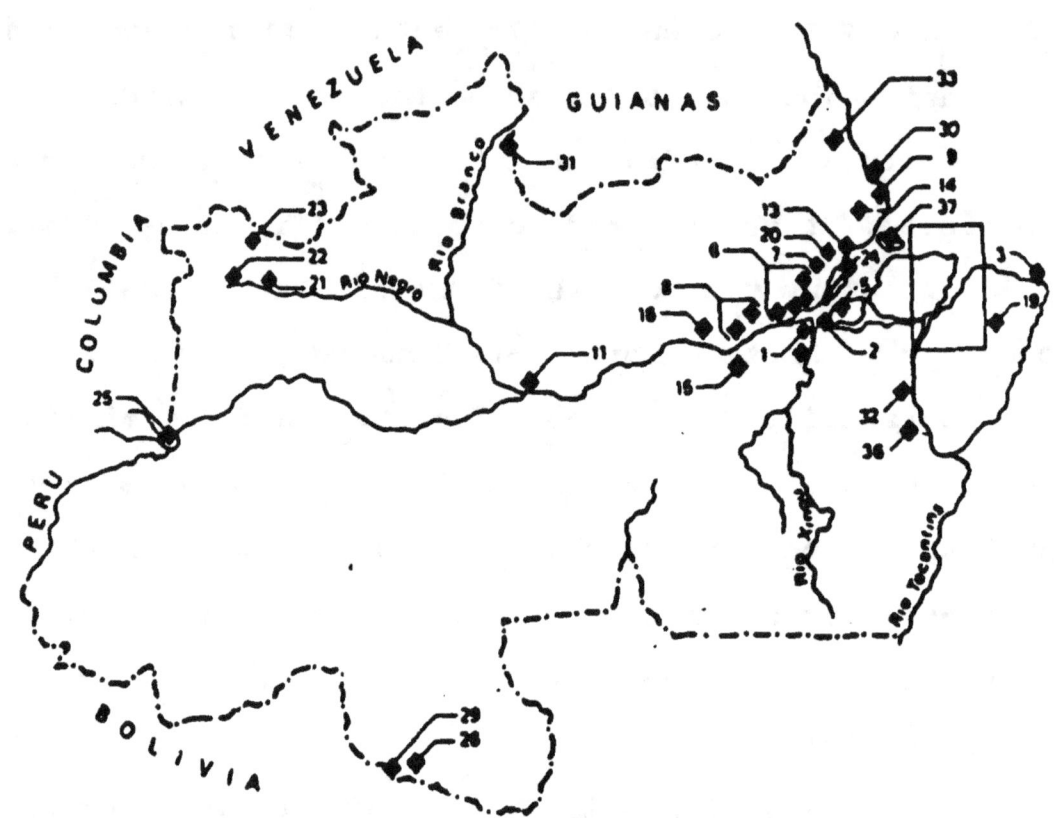

☐ – Area of Fort Belém and vicinity.
1-Forts Orange and Nassau.
2-Fort Mariocai.
3-Forts Cumá and Caeté.
4-Fort Santo Antônio de Gurupá (Gurupá).
5-Forts Murutu, Mandiutuba, Torrego and Felipe.
6-Fort Cumau.
7-Forts Desterro and Teoré.
8-Fort Araguari.
9-Fort S. Pedro Nolasco (Belém).
10-Fort S. José da Barra do Rio Negro (Manaus).
11-Fort da Barra (Belém).
12-Fort Santo Antônio de Macapá.
13-Fort Rio Batabonte.
14-Fort Santarém or Tapajós.
15-Fort Óbidos or de Pauxis.
16-Fort Paru (Almerim).
17-Fort and Battery Periquitos island (Belém).

18-Fort Guamá (Ourem).
19-Fort Curiau.
20-Fort São Gabriel (Uaupés).
21-Fort São Joaquim (Rio Negro).
22-Fort Cucuí (Maribatanas).
23-Fort Macapá.
24-Fort Tabatinga.
25-Fort Nossa Senhora da Conceição.
26-Fort São José (Belém).
27-Battery Val-de-Cans (Belém).
28-Fort Príncipe da Beira.
29-Fort Cabo Norte.
30-Fort São Joaquim.
31-Fort Nossa Senhora de Nazaré (Tucurui).
32-Fort Cabo Norte.
33-Battery Santo Antônio (Belém).
34-Fort Periquitos island (Belém).
35-Fort Itaboca waterfall.
36-Fort Bragança island.

FIGURE 8

In 1900, the President of Switzerland, acting as mediator, awarded Brazil 101,000 square miles of the region called Amapá - in Amazon region - in a dispute with France. Baron Rio Branco's success stemmed from his vast knowledge of the geography of these areas, the history of the disputes over them, and his adherence to the following principles:[40]

o First, he refused to consider the Treaties of Madrid and San Ildefonso more than preliminary statements of Portuguese and Spanish sovereignty; the precise borders continued uncertain and needed further definition,

o Second, the criterion for establishing ownership was *uti possidetis*, whether the territory was occupied predominantly by Portuguese or other language speakers, and

o Third, he favored bilateral negotiations rather than outside arbitration, if possible.

The accompanying map (Figure 9) shows additional territorial settlements - most of them in the Amazon region - with England, Colombia, Peru and Bolivia. By the end of his career, Rio Branco had secured 342,000 square miles for Brazil, an area larger than France.[41]

Once in possession of this land, Brazil's policy was to maintain sovereignty over it. Brazil's capacity to do so was limited by the scanty population, difficult communications, and the length of the border, but neighboring countries were even less capable of settling and fortifying their holdings in the Amazon basin.

RIO BRANCO

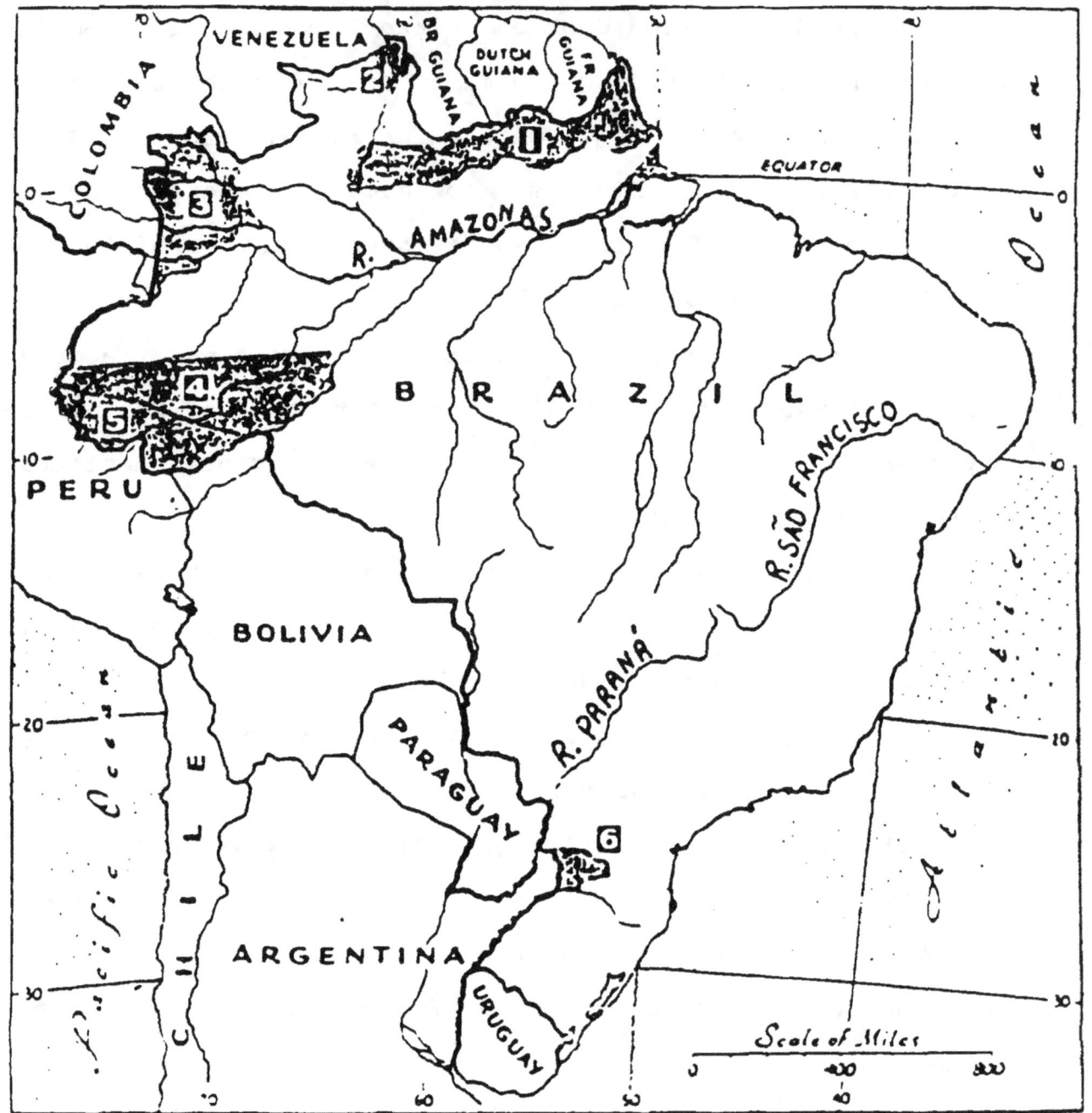

FIGURE 9

1 French Guiana. Territory of Amapa
   Arbitral Award of the Swiss Federal Council. December 1 1900
2 British Guiana
   Arbitral Award of King Victor Emmanuel III of Italy. June 6. 1904
3 Colombia
   Treaty of Limits and Navigation. April 24, 1907
   Clarified by the Treaty of Limits and Navigation. November 15. 1928
4 Peru
   Treaty of Demarcation of Frontiers. September 8. 1909
5 Bolivia. Territory of Acre
   Treaty of Petropolis. November 17. 1903
6 Argentina. Treaty of Missões
   Arbitral Award of President Grover Cleveland of the United States. February 5. 1895

THE GEOPOLITICAL MANEUVER

Brazil has remained united through the genius of its ancestors. This union was consummated on a grand scale in this century through a "Geopolitical Maneuver" that Brazil has been carrying out since the end of World War II.

Prior to the "Geopolitical Maneuver", the Brazilian territory in the 1940's could be described as follows:

-the Central Nucleus -- the "Heart of Brazil",

-the three peninsulas: Northeast, South and Middle-West, and

-the Amazon" island"[42] (Figure 10).

The Central Nucleus was densely populated and developed. The peninsulas were weakly connected to the central nucleus; the Amazon island was isolated and not linked to the rest of the country.

An action program to integrate and settle the national geographic space was imperative. The "Geopolitical Maneuver" to do this was to unfold in three phases, as follows:

- the first phase: to link the Central Nucleus to the South and to the Northeast, was accomplished in the 40's and 50's. It included:

. BR 116 - road linking Rio de Janeiro/Porto Alegre/ Jaguarão,

. BR 116 - road linking Rio de Janeiro/Bahia/Fortaleza,

. railroad to the South, and

. link-up of the Northeast railroad network.

31

GEOPOLITICAL MANEUVER

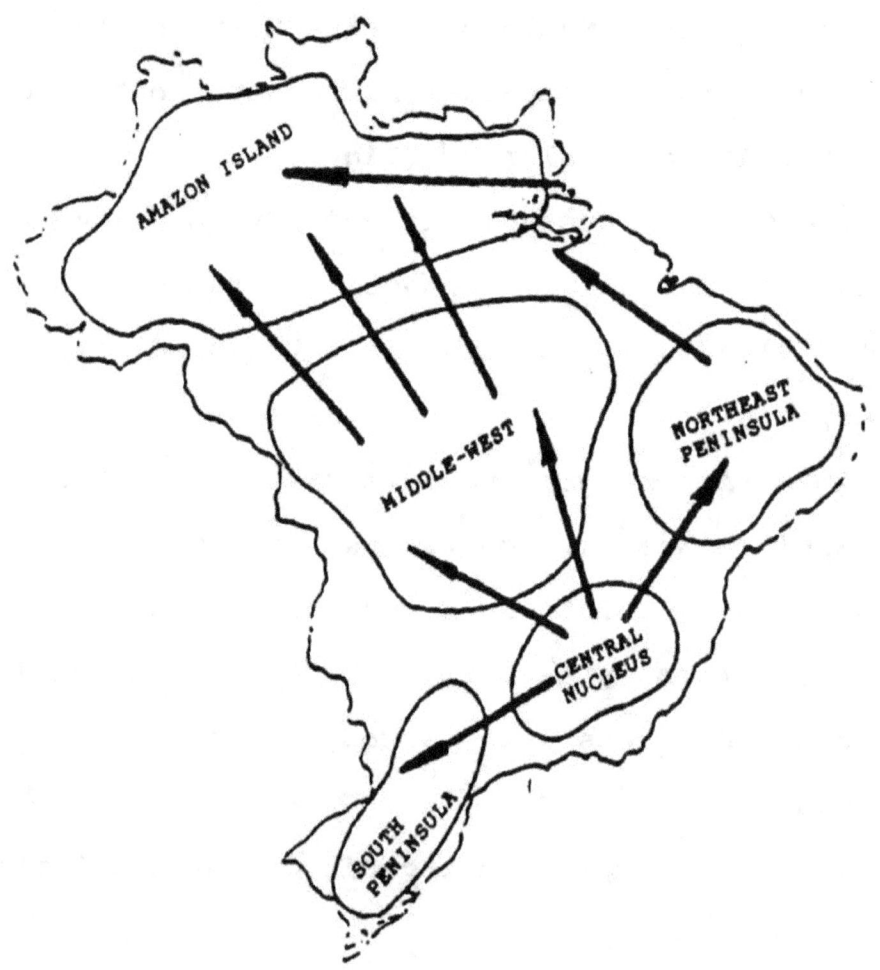

FIGURE 10

- the second phase: to advance to the Middle-West from the
Central Nucleus,was done in the 60's and 70's. It included

. construction of Brasília,

. BR 267 - road linking São Paulo/Mato Grosso,

. BR 040 - Road linking Rio de Janeiro/Brasília/Cuiabá,

. railroad linking Baurú/Corumbá, and

. linking Brasília to the Central Nucleus railroad system.

- the third phase: to link the Amazon" island" to the more
populated regions, is in execution now. The Middle-West was
defined as the advanced base for this conquest, with development
proceeding from east to west along the Amazon river. This phase
includes:

. BR 040 - road linking Belém/Brasília,

. BR 364 - road linking Cuiabá/Porto Velho/Rio Branco/
    Cruzeiro do Sul,

. BR 319 - road linking Porto Velho/Manaus,

. BR 163 - road linking Cuiabá/Santarém, and

. BR 230 - Trans-Amazon Highway (Figure 11).

BRAZIL'S RAIL SYSTEM

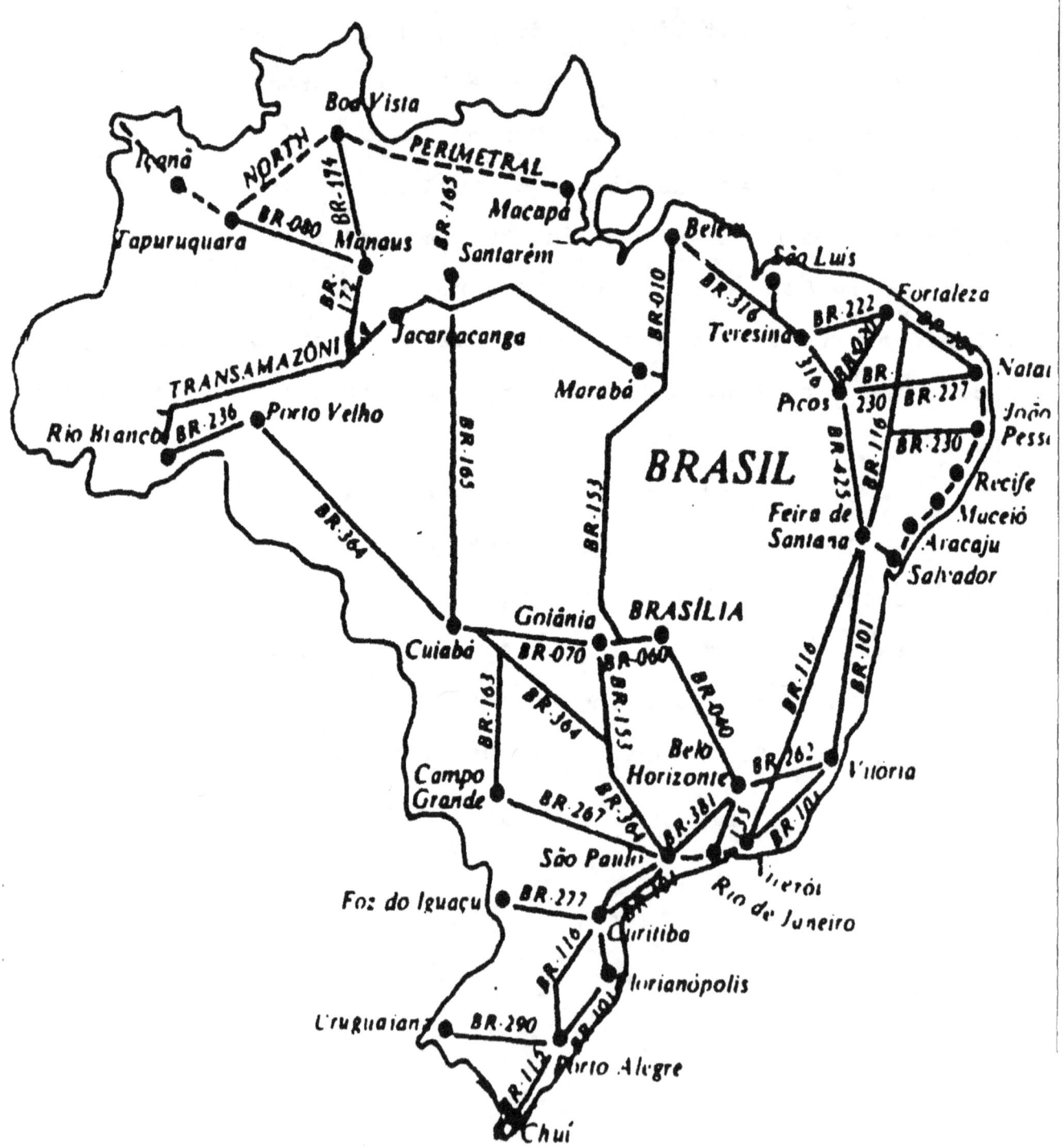

FIGURE 11

THE ISSUE OF THE AMAZON AREA

The Amazon is a region of inestimable potential with some important still-unsolved problems, such as the indian issues, gold prospecting, and the increasingly important issue of narcotics trafficking.

NARCOTICS TRAFFICKING

Narcotrafficking would not be considered a critical issue were it not for the recent associations formed between narcotraffickers and guerrilla groups. These associations have given narcotraffickers more political power and guerrillas more economic power, with the entire process creating conditions conducive to the spread of guerrilla movements. Furthermore, the issue has strategic importance because of the sociological impact of production and consumption of the drug, even though the great consumer centers for drugs are still outside the South American continent.

The main drug-producing countries are Bolivia, Peru, and Colombia, the South American "golden triangle" (Figure 12). However, drugs are a problem in other South American countries, such as Brazil and Venezuela, which are being used as routes for exporting drugs. Drugs could even lay the foundations for narcoterrorism in these countries.[43]

In Peru, there is evidence of an increasing level of cooperation between the guerrilla groups and the

35

MAJOR COCA PRODUCTION AREAS

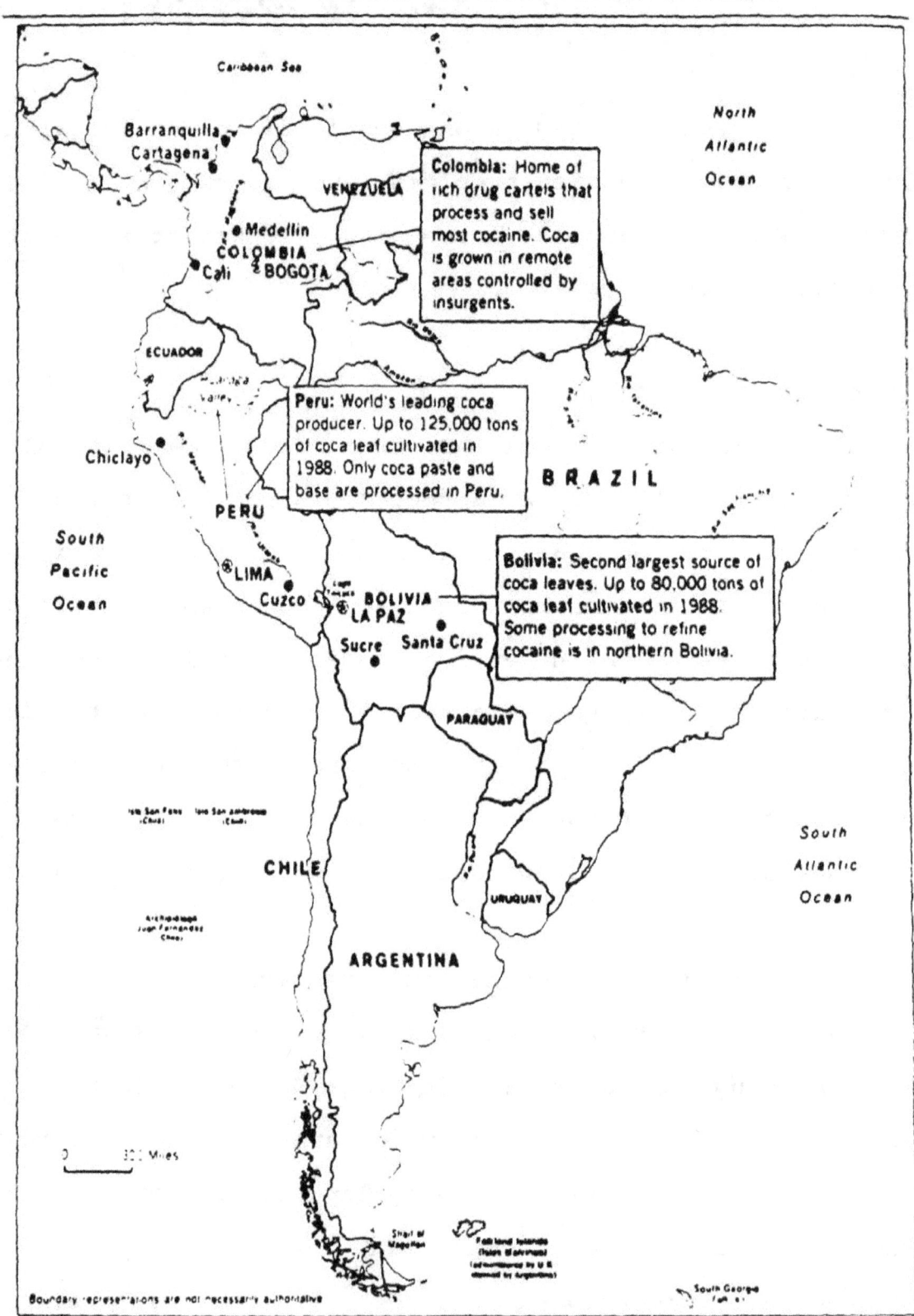

FIGURE 12

narcotraffickers, not only in the mountains but also in the Peruvian Amazon near the Brazilian border.

In Colombia, the union between terrorists and narcotraffickers has given rise to narcoterrorism. The Colombian Amazon region has been used extensively for preparation of drugs, in particular cocaine. Equipment and makeshift laboratories have been installed in the jungle.

In Bolivia, there is a great danger that trafficking in drugs and other contraband, if not repressed in time, will threaten the very political life of the country. Because of Bolivia's central position, this could inevitably affect the neighboring countries.

Ecuador has shown concern about drugs, convinced that narcotrafficking increases the war-waging power and action of guerrilla movements, corrupts and destroys the police force, demoralizes the judicial branch, and undermines the executive branch.

The war against narcotraffickers and the guerrilla groups pursued by Colombia, Peru, and Bolivia with support from the United States, has increased the interest of narcotraffickers and guerrillas in Brazil. The United States pressures Brazil to use its Armed Forces in the war on drugs, but according to the present Brazilian Constitution, the Armed Forces cannot be used in this way; that mission is the exclusive responsibility of the Brazilian Federal Police and the Military Police authorities of the Brazilian states.[44]

On the other hand, the Brazilian chamber of deputies commission for congressional investigation, CPI, wants the Armed Forces to participate in the war on drugs at the Brazilian border with the Andean countries. The Brazilian border with Venezuela, Peru, Bolivia and Colombia is more than 6,250 miles long. Also, the CPI wants to implement the Live Hedge operation by 1992. The operation's objective is to reinforce border control and prevent drugtrafficking in Brazil.[45] The Armed Forces' role in the operation would be to supervise and support the Brazilian Federal Police. The Federal Police role would undoubtedly be to arrest the drugtraffickers.

On Jun 12 1991, the Brazilian Congress approved the text of the 1988 United Nations Convention against Illicit Traffic in Narcotic Drugs and Psychotropic Substances. Having thus met the domestic constitutional requirements, the Brazilian Government is now nearing final ratification of the Convention. Even before ratification, the Brazilian authorities have been carrying out a broad range of actions in the field of drug law enforcement in accordance with the objectives of the 1988 U.N. Convention. Ratification will constitute an important step in the process of consolidating and strengthening actions against illegal drug traffic.[46]

Finally, the Constitution of Brazil devotes many specific provisions to the drug problem. In the Congress, a parliamentary group has been established to deal with legislative issues pertaining to drug abuse control. This group, in cooperation with the Federal Council on Narcotics, has recently submitted a bill updating the anti-drug legislation of 1976. As required by the Constitution, Congress has also recently enacted legislation establishing drugtrafficking as a most serious criminal offense.

THE GOLD MINING ISSUE

Because of its huge territorial expanse and its varied resources, the Amazon has been the principal target of mining disputes. The mineral-rich and therefore most economically important part of the Amazon region, unfortunately, is found in indian areas. This has provoked an invasion of gold-miners into indian areas, with attendant disruption of indian cultures.

In addition, gold prospecting has been carried out with great intensity along the border, especially in Amapá, Roraima, Amazonas and Rondônia states, creating incidents with French Guiana, Venezuela, Colombia, and Bolivia.

The most promising areas for gold mining are either encumbered by applications for exploration or are in indian areas. Jostling for these areas gives rise to conflicts that pit gold-miners against mining companies, gold-miners against indians, and mining companies against indians. Generally, the most prevalent conflicts are between gold-miners and mining companies and between gold-miners and indians.

An associated problem is the flow of contraband metals and precious stones over the border into neighboring countries. From 1986 to 1989, the amount of illegal production of gold was extremely large: 39.6% and 65% respectively, of the total production.[47] Problems associated with gold mining potentially disturb internal order, harm relations with neighboring countries, and project a negative image of Brazil's indian and environmental policies.

THE INDIAN SITUATION

The Amazon region, with about 137,000 indians, has 62% of Brazil's indian population.

Brazil's National Foundation for the Indian (FUNAI) estimates a total population of around 230 thousand indians in all of Brazil; of these 10,000 to 15,000 have never been contacted by the authorities. FUNAI identifies 467 known indian areas in Brazil, occupying 520,000 square miles, or 10% of the Brazilian territory.[48] Thus, each Brazilian indian (including children) has, on average, an area of 400 hectares in which to live. By comparison, an indian in the United States lives on only 18 hectares.[49]

The Brazilian "indian question" is the subject of disinformation and deliberate mystification. Some, for example, The 1987 New State of the World Atlas maintains that, in Brazil, "The indians have been bombed, poisoned, and deliberately infected with tuberculosis, influenza and smallpox.[50] Although it is clear that there have been cases of violence against indians in Brazil, these have been isolated incidents, nearly always involving gold miners or cattlemen. Public opinion, both in

Brazil and internationally, has been too often manipulated by special groups who have tried to portray the Brazilian government as well as many miners and cattlemen as being indian killers or predators of nature.[51]

The indians' situation is difficult due to their precarious conditions of life, but they have never before enjoyed such widespread sympathy among the mainstream society, both inside and outside Brazil. International orchestration of this issue, now truly a universal clamor, seeks the formation of "Indian Nations".[52] Whatever the motivation for this clamor, the creation of sovereign indian nations would form unwanted enclaves that could threaten Brazilian integrity and cause economic damage.

Thus, the indian issue, at present, involves Brazilian national sovereignty, touches on the external debt issue, tends to advance the internationalization of the Amazon area, and is connected to the issue of environment.

THE GENETIC CORNUCOPIA

Today, one of the greater dangers in the Amazon rain forest is the possible destruction of the richest genetic pool in the world, whose potential benefit to mankind is yet undiscovered.

There are solid reasons to preserve the forest's physical integrity and to use it only for economic activities that are the least harmful possible to its plant cover. The strongest of these reasons is the luxuriant proliferation of life within the jungle.

There is no accurate estimate of the number of species

living on the planet. In the 1960s, estimates were around three million species. Today, one might consider five million, and there are those who estimate to 10 million. In the Amazon alone, some observers estimate that around two million species have their habitat in the jungle; of these, only 30% or so are known by scientists.[53]

The Amazon jungle is so dense and teeming with life that all the biologists on earth could not fully describe the life forms it supports. Agronomists see the forest as a cornucopia of undiscovered food sources, and chemists scour the flora and fauna for compounds with seemingly magical properties. The number of plants with medicinal value has already been estimated at around 4,000.[54] The actual number, however, might be much higher. Thus, one finds in the Amazon from one-fifth to one-third of all genetic wealth of the world. This is one of the forest's biggest resources, and is as valuable as the mineral resources that exist underground.

One of the aims of research on vegetable and animal species of the Amazonian region is to try to find new drugs. For instance, jungle chemicals have already led to new treatments for hypertension and some forms of cancer. In fact, at least 25% of all chemical products of the world contain materials that come from the rain forests.[55]

Another of the rain forest's genetic riches is its biodiversity. A 1982 U.S. National Academy of Sciences report estimated that the Amazonian rain forest contains more than

60,000 species of plants, 2,000 species of fish, more than 300 species of mammals, 11% of the birds of the world, and an undetermined number of microscopic forms of life.[56] The Amazon may also contain many still-undiscovered natural insecticides and solutions to many of the world's other problems. For example, the piquia tree produces a compound that appears to be toxic to leaf-cutter ants that cause millions of dollars of damage each year to South America agriculture. Such chemicals promise attractive alternatives to dangerous synthetic pesticides.

On the other hand, scientists also calculate that thirty unknown species are disappearing every day from the Amazon. The rate of destruction of living species is 500 times greater than the natural rate of evolution.[57]

This is the genetic treasure that needs to be studied thoroughly for the benefits that it can bring to humanity. The greatest importance of the forest is its role as a genetic resource. The lessons encoded in the genes of the Amazon's plants and animals may ultimately hold the key to solving a wide range of human problems. Clearly, any plan for substantial development of the economic potential of the Amazon must recognize and preserve the region's biological wealth.

Biological resources are a basic component of the national heritage of the countries to which they belong. The respect for the sovereignty of States over these resources should form the basis for any international action involving the conservation and sustainable use of biological diversity.

43

BURNING AND DEFORESTATION

As in other countries, the industrialization process in Brazil was not initially disciplined in the application of appropriate environmental safeguards. Urban growth was accompanied by rapid expansion in the use of land for agricultural activities. In 25 years, the total area used for agriculture increased from 230 million to 320 million hectares.[58] The process of opening up new areas was expanded haphazardly until it reached the Amazonian region.

That rapid expansion sped up the deforestation rate. Until 1975, 2.8 million hectares had been deforested in the Legal Amazonia; that increased to 7.7 million hectares by 1978. Two years later, 12.5 million hectares had been deprived of their forest cover, a figure that grew to 59.8 million hectares in 1988 (according to World Bank estimates). In 1987 alone, 20 million hectares were burnt, of which 12 million hectares were land used for pasture and agriculture or covered by second growth, and 8.0 million hectares were native forests.[59]

The 1987 data, however were based on pictures taken from the NOAA satellite, which is primarily used for weather purposes and has a 1000-meter resolution level (better data could have come from the LANDSAT satellite, which has 30-meter resolution).[60] Nevertheless, the deforestation figures released for 1987 shocked Brazil and the world.

The deforested area within Amazonia varies between 5% and 10%, depending on the reference time period and geographic area.

Brazil's National Institute of Spatial Research (INPE) tries to assert a fundamental difference between clearing (deforestation) and burning. This is based on the concept that all deforestation represent a use of the land, whereas not every burning is associated with deforestation. The peripheral agricultural areas of the tropical rain forest, for example, consist of savannahs and border vegetation; they have been burnt annually by small local farmers for a quite long time, and this does not constitute an aggression against the forest.

The government of Brazil has taken strong steps recently to curb environmental degradation. The new Constitution, promulgated on October 5, 1988, devoted a whole chapter to the issue. One of its provisions makes the existence of ecological reserves and parks compulsory in the states and municipalities, referring to any environment-harming activity as a "crime".[61]

As it works to sustain rational, responsible development of the Amazon proper, the Brazilian government continues to deal with several challenges. For the remaining intact areas, which correspond to over 90% of the Amazon region, the government must apply a policy of rational use, environmental conservation, and protection of both indian communities and local populations.

Only in the last year has the government succeeded in diminishing the problems of burnings and deforestation, showing a decrease of approximately 30% in comparison to 1988.[62] This decrease was due not only to the combined environmental protection and awareness campaigns carried out by the Brazilian

Environment and Renewable Resources Institute (IBAMA), but also to the fact that prospecting activities attracted labor that would otherwise have been employed in the removal of forest cover.

Aggressions against nature in the Amazon have decreased noticeably. IBAMA has prohibited, for instance, the exploitation of lumber, an activity which until recently allowed a yearly export of thousands of cubic meters of raw material to foreign markets. In so doing, IBAMA halted the flow of noble species endangered by extinction, which were being sold at low prices on the international market.

THE THREATS

WHY THE AMAZON?

Why has the Amazon region been a target of so much interest and discussion, to the point of involving almost the whole world?

One could ask:

o Could the resources of the Amazon be coveted by numerous outside interest groups?

o What are the intentions of these interest groups?

o What can possibly exist in the Amazon to justify external interests to such a degree as to put the integrity of Brazilian territorial integrity at risk?

o Is the Amazon really sort of a world lung?

o Are the fires that are claimed to be taking place in the area aggravating the greenhouse effect?

o Is there danger that extensive areas in the Amazon may become desert?

o Can hydroelectric power plants of large and medium size cause ecologic damage to the area?

o Have the interests of the indigenous populations been prejudiced by the development process in the Amazon?

o Why is the attention of the world's environmentalists focused on the Amazon?

ATTEMPTS AT INTERFERENCE IN THE PAST

Perhaps one should start consideration of these questions with the last point above.

Interest groups and/or nations have attempted to interfere in the Amazon area for a long time; one must know something of the history of that interference to understand present events.

Throughout the 17th century, French, English, and Dutch explorers tried to hold on to certain areas of the Amazon and exploit the timber market; but they were always expelled.

After Brazilian political independence in 1822, international pressures mounted to assure free navigation through the rivers of the Amazon. The Amazon Navigation Company of the USA was the first to test freedom of navigation on the Amazon. The arrival of the company's first ship in the area caused widespread confusion. The ship was not allowed to use the river, and tremendous diplomatic pressure was brought to bear on Brazil.

In the USA, Brazil was alleged to be committing a crime against humanity because it was preventing foreign ships from using the Amazonic rivers and thereby "bringing civilization" to the region.[63]

In 1850, Lieutenant Matthew Fontaine Maury of the U.S. Navy, an astronomer at the National Observatory in Washington who also headed the Navy's hydrographic services, started a campaign to internationalize the Amazon. Repercussions from this campaign reached the most important European countries.[64]

In articles in the principal North American newspapers of the time, and also in his book "The Amazon Rivers and the Atlantic Slopes of the South America", Lieutenant Maury said that the Amazon should not be closed to humanity. In a report to his government he said: "The Amazon is waiting for strong and resolute races to conduct its scientific and economic conquest."[65]

The same Matthew Maury also wrote an article for "Bow's Review" in which he suggested that the Gulf of Mexico and the Amazon are part of the same geographical complex and, in consequence, the Amazon should be considered an extension of the Mississippi. This theory triggered a later proposal to create an Amazonic Republic to protect the American blacks freed from slavery.[66]

At the end of the nineteenth century, the "Bolivian Syndicate" was set up in New York to negotiate a deal with the Bolivian Government to occupy a province that was, at the time, a disputed area between Brazil and Bolivia.[67]

In 1902 the German foreign minister, Baron Oswald Richtofen, asserted to the chief of the Brazilian delegation in Germany, Baron Rio Branco, that, "It would be convenient that Brazil not prevent the rest of the world from sharing in the natural amazonic wealth."[68]

Also at that time, the U.S. Secretary of State, John Hay, told Brazilian Ambassador Assis Brasil in Washington that he "could not see any risk to the sovereignty of the American nations from the setting up of industrial companies to develop uncultivated lands".[69] The intent was to press Brazil into allowing the famous "Chartered Companies" into its territory, the very method that had been used to "colonize" Africa.[70]

After World War II, a new campaign was launched by the Brazilian scientist, Paulo Berredo Carneiro, with support from UNESCO, to found the International Institute of Amazonic Hylea. The goal was to establish an international council powerful enough to decide what could and what could not be done in the region.[71]

Finally, in the 1960s, the Hudson Institute launched the huge "Great Amazon Lake" project or "Plan of the Amazonic Mediterranean Sea", which foresaw the building of seven great lakes in the Amazon. The greatest of these lakes, to be formed by dams with 30 to 50 million kilowatts of electric generating capacity, was to facilitate riverine navigation from Brazil to other Amazonian countries. According to Robert Panero, Hudson

Institute's engineer, the lakes would connect the river basins in Brazil. Something equivalent would be made in Chocó, Colombia. The two systems would ultimately be joined by a system of canals, allowing ships to enter at the mouth of the Amazon, transit the Continent, and exit to the Pacific through Colombia. This would be an alternative to the Panama Canal. The Brazilian government rejected this idea.[72]

THE NEW ATTEMPT - THE REAL AIM

External threats and international greed remain today. However, they are often disguised and carried out in a more intelligent and efficient way, by some groups that use arguments -- ecology and preservation of the indian culture -- which powerfully touch world public opinion, and are supported by an intense and systematic campaign by the media.

Could there be something more than mere concern for better conditions of life on Earth behind the interest expressed in the Amazon by so many "ecologists"?

The tendency of countries of great politico-economic power to try to keep the status-quo, which they call "world stability", can be considered nowadays as nothing more than attempts to freeze their relative advantages in order to guarantee better the living standards for their populations. It is exactly this issue that blocks the attempts by emerging nations', including Brazil, to succeed in their development efforts. To support Brazilian development, the developed countries would have to place at risk

50

interests already "established" and markets already "defined".
Emergence of a new strong player would certainly affect
distribution of markets and power, with natural and unpredictable
losses for those players currently satisfied with their present
situation.[73] The question remains, however; how could the Amazon
upset the equilibrium already achieved?

The last remaining virgin areas on Earth capable of
providing their exploiters with additional economic advantage are
as follows:

- the Arctic areas of Canada, Greenland, and Russia,

- the Antarctic, and

- the Amazon

Considering that the frigid areas are difficult to exploit
economically despite all the recent technological advances, and
that exploitation of the Antarctic is precluded by treaty for the
foreseeable future, the Amazon remains as the only potential
source of great additional wealth and power to its exploiters.

Previously, nations took part in wild and unruly competition
to project their power over other nations' territory. Everything
was considered quite correct, even becoming legalized through
international treaties. Although all past attempts at external
interference in the Amazon have failed, one cannot rule out
continued competition.

There is no doubt about the area's economic potential; that
has been registered by satellites. If rationally exploited, the
forest could be an important renewable source of wood.

The Amazon's reserves of gold, aluminum, tin, manganese, niobium and wolfram are immense. The hydroelectric potential of the Amazon could guarantee power for virtually any economic endeavor. The possibilities of the region for development of biotechnology are so obvious they need no further elaboration.

In my judgment "One cannot let all this power be exploited solely by the Brazilian people" was probably in the minds of those who began the international publicity campaign on Amazonian development.

THE ACTORS AND THEIR INTERESTS

A retrospective analysis and study of the present state of affairs leads to the identification of the following as the main characters playing in the Amazon affair, with their associated interests:

1. **The Government of Brazil**: it is the main actor and principal target of the other actors' actions. Its interests in the area are:

    - to reach and maintain its Permanent National Objectives (ONP -- "Objetivos Nacionais Permanentes"),[74]

    - to promote socio-economic development in the Amazon, without damaging the balance of the Amazonian ecosystems, in order to transform the country into a power with a high standard of living,

    - to maintain Brazilian sovereignty over the area,

    - to establish strategic outlets to the Pacific and the

Caribbean -- through partnerships and cooperative
endeavors between Brazil and its Amazonian neighbors
and in accordance with the objectives of the "Pan-
Amazon Treaty" -- in order to increase trade with the
Asian countries and Brazil's presence in the
Caribbean area (Figure 13),

- to deal fairly with the indigenous communities in
  accordance with the Constitution,

- to eliminate, or at least minimize, the actions of drug
  traffickers, preventing their expansion into
  Brazilian territory,

- to organize and control the activities of gold
  prospectors, cattle-ranchers, lumbermen and farmers,
  in order to reduce their effects on the area's
  ecology,

- to promote the socio-economic integration of the
  various Amazonian countries, and

- to respect the rights to self-determination of each
  nation, with the absolute non-acceptance of foreign
  interference of any kind in Brazil's internal affairs.

2. **Other Amazonian countries**: secondary targets of the
actions, they are seeking to achieve and maintain their own ONPs
(permanent aims), eliminate drug trafficking, and preclude
Brazilian hegemony in the area.

3. **Political, economic and scientific groups of developed
"first-world" countries**: they are applying pressure on Brazil

ROAD NETWORK, PAVED AND PROJECTED IN THE AMAZON AREA

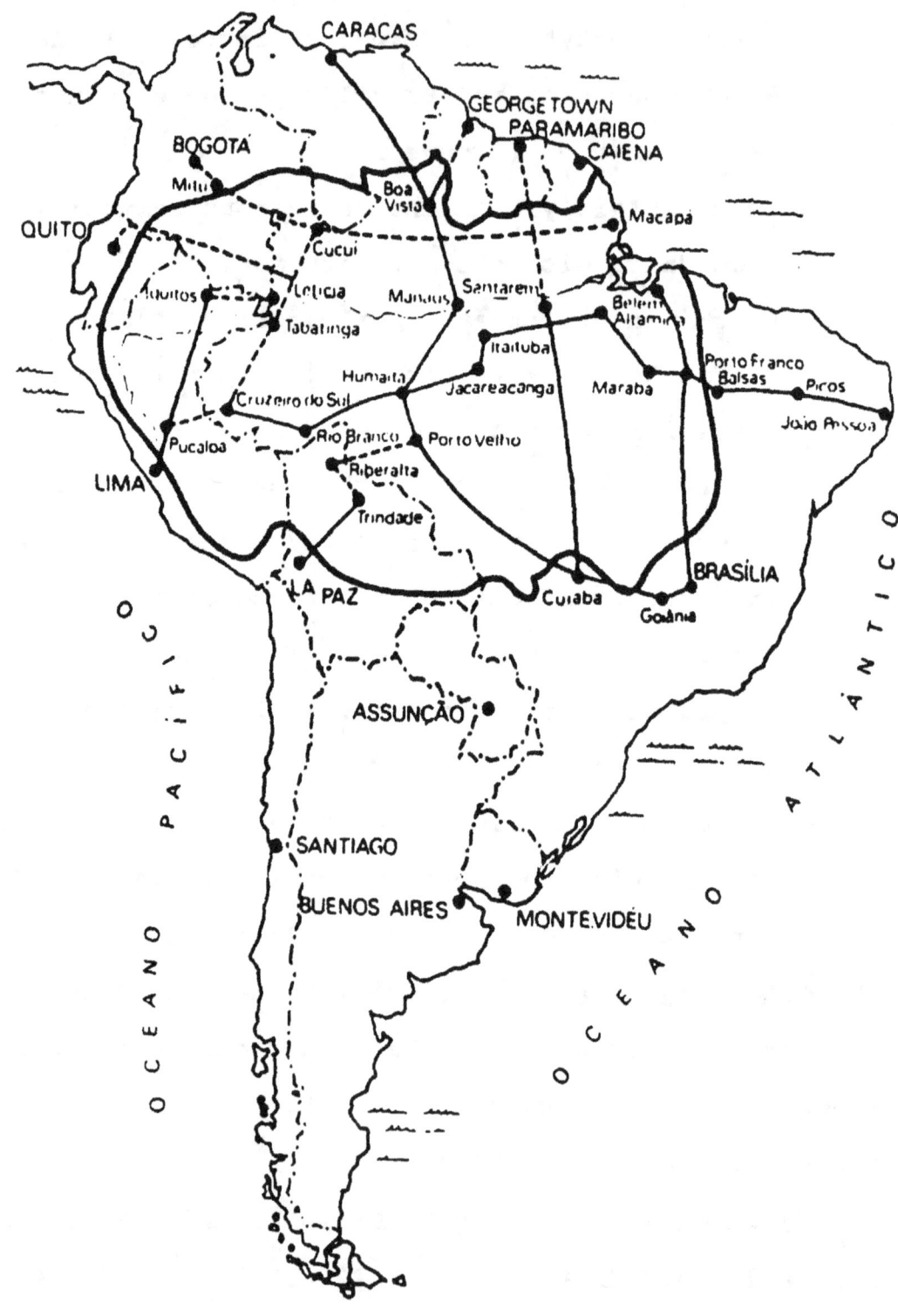

FIGURE 13

according to their individual interests (for example, by opposing loans for Brazil in international development banks). The interests of these countries include:

- preserving "world stability", meaning the _status-quo_ of distribution of power and markets in the world,

- acquiring a share in the exploration and exploitation of the Amazon,

- promoting, if possible, the "internationalization" of the Amazon,

- eliminating narcotrafficking, and

- limiting the influence of other countries' economic groups in Brazil.

4. **Drug Traffickers**: Solidly based in Colombia, Peru, and Bolivia, they manufacture, trade, and export narcotics. They use Brazil as a transit area for narcotrafficking.

5. **Gold prospectors, ranchers, lumbermen and farmers**: with their profit-motivated behavior, they have damaged the area's ecology and given substance to the interventionists' thesis. They have sought to exploit the Amazon with minimum restrictions and control from the Brazilian government.

The following also must also be considered actors interested in the area:

6. **Environmental organizations**: represent the part of the world population genuinely concerned with the planet's future, but are also susceptible to manipulation by the political, economic, and scientific groups of the "first-world". They have

sought to preserve the Amazon as an ecological sanctuary, but also must keep the support of governments and institutions that sustain them economically and politically.

7. **The Media**: with remarkable worldwide concerted action (particularly by the developed countries) against Brazil, they nurture a clear tendency in their populations to support any action, regardless of its nature, so long as it is labeled as the solution to the ecological problem. They have sought to maintain their influence and prestige, manipulate public opinion, and represent the interests of ideological or economic groups.

8. **Catholic clergy**: with a strong hold over the humble people of the Amazon's remote areas, they are powerful enough to influence them and exploit the "whites against indians" conflict to create indigenous nations whose sovereignty can then be "internationalized".

9. **Humble Population (including indian minorities)**: although not totally integrated into today's Brazilian life, they are likely to be influenced and used. They have sought to preserve their culture and traditions and to have adequate areas (reservations) where they would not be economically exploited.

The above list presents merely the more important actors; it could be enlarged depending on the level of analysis desired.

PERTINENCE OF THE CAMPAIGN

Despite the unmistakable international maneuvers to preclude exploitation of the Amazon by Brazil alone and to press for

internationalization of the area, one should check whether the
allegations made against Brazil are true or pertinent.

This paper will provide answers to five questions or
allegations of international interest; these will help clarify
the campaign waged by the related actors today. The questions,
and related discussions, are as follows:

1."*Is the Amazon really a kind of world lung?*"

No. Anyone who studies plant ecology knows that while they
grow, plants produce much more oxygen than they consume and,
thus, enrich the environment. The Amazon, however, has already
reached its climax and when this happens, almost all oxygen
produced during the day is consumed through plant respiration and
oxidation of dead vegetable matter.

The Amazon has an amazing potential to produce oxygen but,
ironic as it may seem, part of its fully-developed vegetation
must be cut down to exploit the potential. It may not be
necessary, after all, to manipulate oxygen production in the
Amazon; the proportion of oxygen in the air globally has remained
at a steady level over the last several centuries, on average
20.95%.[75]

In fact, it is the sea and not the forest that actually
provides the oxygen that one breathes in the world; the sea does
this through its plankton, phytoplankton and various ocean micro-
organisms.

2."*Is the burning that today is taking place in the Amazon aggravating the greenhouse effect?*"

The greenhouse effect is an expression which makes a comparison between that which happens in the atmosphere and which occurs in glasshouses where, in countries having colder climates, flowers and vegetables are cultivated. In greenhouses, the light penetrates the transparent glass, heating the interior, at which point the heat cannot escape because the glass is a thermic isolator. In the same way, heat created with burning of carbon dioxide (CO_2) remains trapped in the highest layers of the atmosphere, causing global warming of the Earth.[76]

According to the scientists Antonio Tebaldi Tardin and Luiz Gylvan Meira Filho of the Brazilian Institute for Space Research (INPE), Brazil produces, due to burnings in the Amazon region, close to 300 million tons of carbon dioxide emissions per year. On the other hand, industrialized countries emit over 5 billion tons of carbon dioxide each year, through factory chimneys and automobiles emissions. Therefore, the contribution of the burnings in the Amazon to the greenhouse effect is of little consequence (about 1%).[77]

Even considering the burnings and deforestation of all the earth's tropical forests, taking place in Laos, Nigeria, Colombia, and others, a total of 1.5 billion tons per year would be reached, a total much lower than the amount generated by the industrialized nations, those truly responsible for the greenhouse effect.[78]

This phenomenon is potentially extremely dangerous because it could melt the polar ice caps, thus flooding many coastal cities throughout the world. Man is also responsible for a second important cause of the greenhouse effect. Chlorofluorcarbons (CFC), present in aerosols, result in the destruction of the atmosphere's ozone layer. Therefore, it is wrong to attribute a majority of the responsibility for the possible heating of the Earth in the future to the present burning of the Amazon forest.

3. *"Is there a risk that extensive areas of the Amazon forest will become desert areas?"*

This hypothesis lacks scientific evidence. For desertification to take place, a considerable climatic change would be necessary, especially alterations of wind cycles.

There is no study so far that shows any possibility that this could happen. To the contrary, studies carried out in the Amazon jungle revealed that the forest has grown back rapidly in all burnout areas as well as in other areas where deforestation has taken place.

In fact, there is some risk of soil degradation, but even that can only happen in areas where the forest is used without adequate agronomic technology.

4. *"Could medium-and larger-sized hydroelectric plants cause serious ecological damage to the Amazon?"*

The problem of ecological damage must be understood in terms relative to the entire national territory.

All the hydroelectric plants planned to be completed by 2010 will flood only 0.2% of the Amazon area. What does 0.2% mean? Thinking about it in relative terms, it means nothing.[79]

Persons not familiar with the vastness of Brazil -- in particular Amazonia -- are sometimes easily impressed with data they receive. For instance, the Italian Army Chief of Staff told of his concern some time ago, when he heard that an area the size of Sicily had been burned in the Amazon.[80] What is Sicily? The size of Sicily compared to Brazil is nothing.

An economy such as Brazil's cannot be ruled by the liberal side of the ecological movement. The same people who are fighting against the hydroelectric plants are also against the nuclear plants. What suitable alternative do they have to meet the demand for energy in a country like Brazil, with such an increasing rate of development?

5. *"Have the indigenous populations been prejudiced by the development process in the Amazon?"*

The Brazilian indian affair has been discussed at the international level. For many years, however, Brazil has been developing a policy for preserving the cultures and improving the living conditions of the indigenous communities, and has even accelerated defense of the interests of the indigenous populations.

The Brazilian government has paid particular attention to this concern over the past few years. In order to defend the interests of, and preserve the indigenous communities, the government has accelerated the demarcation of their lands.

On November 15, 1991 the President of Brazil announced the demarcation of a reserve for the Yanomami Indians. This reservation will allow the Yanomamis to hunt, fish, and celebrate their rites, and thus preserve their way of life. The Yanomami reservation covers an area of 95,000 square kilometers in the states of Amazonas and Roraima, near the Venezuelan border. This reservation is the size of Portugal.[81]

OBSTACLES TO PROTECTING THE AMAZON

The first step in defining a strategy is to address the obstacles to the Amazon area and determine how they complicate attainment of the Brazilian Permanent National Objectives (ONPs) for the area. These obstacles are, generally, the behavior of the actors listed before as they try to accomplish their goals.

Those obstacles are as follows:

o activities of the drug traffickers,

o actions taken by some Amazonian countries against development and integration of the Brazilian economy for fear of contributing to Brazilian hegemony over the area,

o financial restrictions by international organizations as a consequence of external pressures,

o economic retaliation by political, economic, and scientific groups of developed countries,

61

o restrictive political action in international
organizations by the same actors,

o restriction of the access by Brazil to the legitimate
benefits of modern science and technology,

o predatory, illicit economic exploitation by gold
prospectors, ranchers, lumbermen and farmers,

o pressure by environmental organizations to prevent socio-
economic development of the area,

o promotion by part of the clergy of the creation of
indigenous nations,

o the media's influence over national Brazilian and
international public opinion about the Brazilian
government's solution to the Amazon,

o the existence of old laws in Brazilian legislation that
support predatory economic activities,

o present stage of development of the area,

o vastness of the rain forest,

o difficulties in ground communication within the area,

o internal Brazilian regional economic differences which
tend to cause migration flows,

o difficulties of access to the Pacific and the Caribbean,

o the adverse Brazilian economic and financial situation,
and

o the area's low demographic density.

STRATEGIES FOR THE AREA'S SECURITY

CURRENT STRATEGY - THE CALHA NORTE PROJECT

The Calha Norte (Northern Headwaters) project is the most important government effort underway today to promote the region's socio-economic development and integrate the region with the rest of the country.

The Calha Norte project is located to the north of the Solimões and Amazon rivers and covers 4,100 miles of border that separates Brazil from the Guyanas, Suriname, Venezuela, and Colombia (Figure 14). The project involves a 100 mile-wide strip along those borders, or an area of 700,000 square miles; this is equivalent to a quarter of Legal Amazonia and about 15% of Brazil's territory. Within that strip, which runs from Oiapoque in Amapá state to Tabatinga in the Amazonas state, live 1.2 million people, a high percentage of them indians. The strip also contains important mineral resources.[82]

Although the Calha Norte project area has the same characteristics as the Amazon as a whole, it has prominence because of internal and external issues. Internally, a substructure to begin the area's development is lacking. Externally, the problem is how to determine the exact location of the border, an issue that could lead to international frictions. Also, the presence of guerrilla groups from Colombia and drug-traffickers close to the border require that Brazil increase its military presence in that area.

63

CALHA NORTE PROJECT

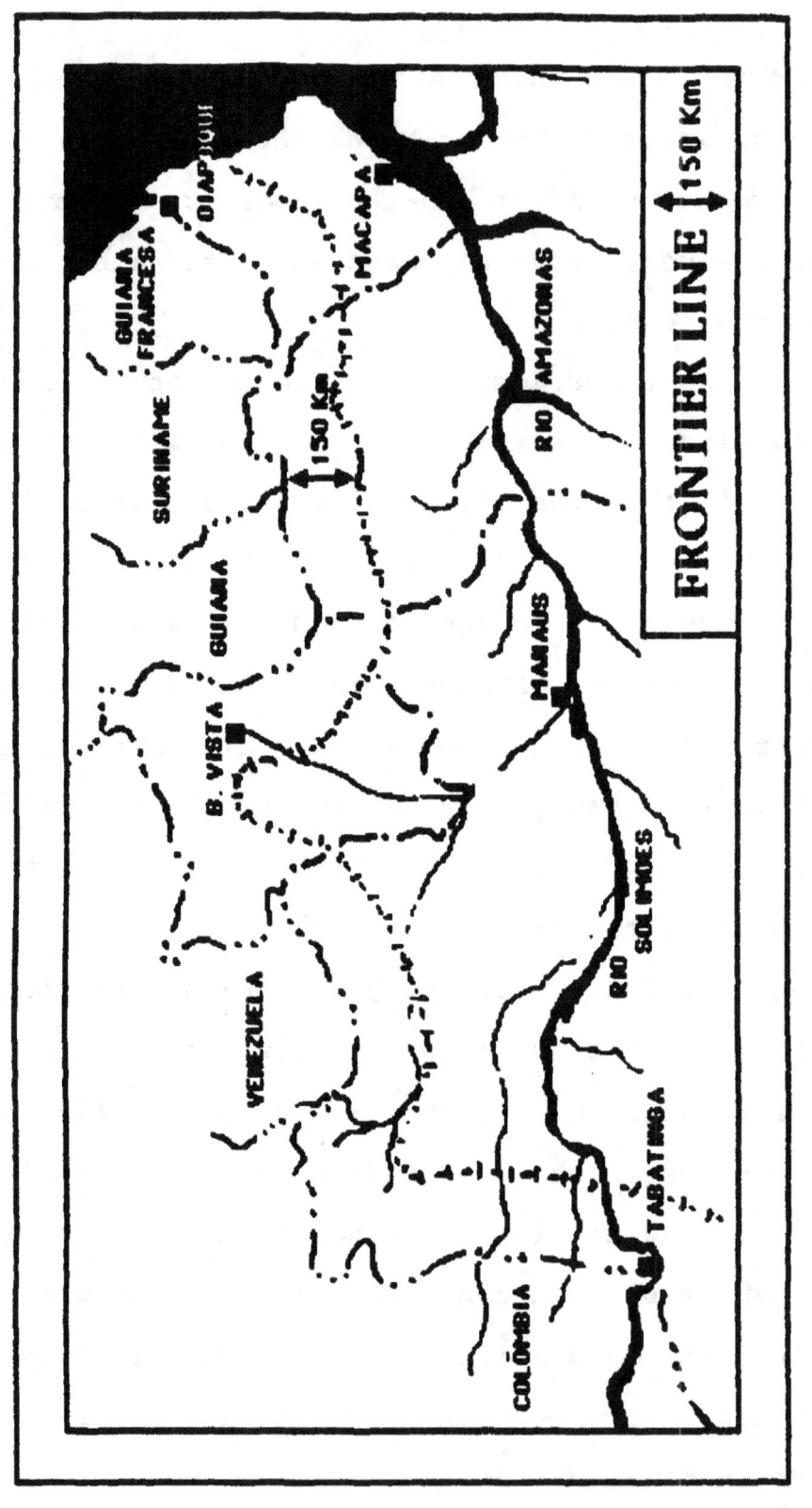

FIGURE 14

The Calha Norte, conceived by the now-defunct National Security Commission, gained visibility in October 1986 when the José Sarney administration released 1.3 billion cruzados ($25 million) -- Brazil's currency at the time -- to finance its implementation along the entire northern border with Amazonia.[83]

The Calha Norte project was created to solve the issues related above, to wit:

o   to intensify bilateral relations, especially economic ones, with the neighboring countries,

o   to increase Brazil's military presence in the area,

o   to expand the consular services network in the area,

o   to intensify the actions of Brazil's National Foundation for the Indian (FUNAI) among the indigenous population,

o   to demarcate the area's boundaries,

o   to stem the loss of foreign exchange caused by flow of contraband metals and precious stones over the border,

o   to combat drug-trafficking, and preclude use of the region as a transit area for narcotics,

o   to move civilians in to settle the area,

o   to develop basic social resources, and

o   to build economic development centers.[85]

The Calha Norte project, through all its phases, was to support development process in the Amazon without destroying the basic ecological characteristics of the region.

The military departments were tasked to increase Brazilian presence over the boundaries and, through engineering projects, to establish a basic infrastructure supporting the region's development. The Brazilian Army had to:

1. create the 1ˢᵗ Jungle Infantry Brigade in Boa Vista - Roraima,

2. reorganize and re-equip the Rio Negro ("Black River"), Roraima, Amapá and Solimões Border Commands,

3. create the 5ᵗʰ Special Border Battalion in São Gabriel da Cachoeira, and

4. create border platoons (see below) in Iauretê, Querari, São Joaquim, Maturacá, Surucucú, Auaris, Ericó (in the Yanomami reservation), and Tiriós (Figure 15).

Border Platoons

Border platoons have 80 men and their installations are prefabricated, transported by river or aircraft from Manaus to their destinations. Also, the platoons are the beginning of new towns. They attract men with their families and provide them energy, water, schools, communications, medical assistance, transport, food, and security. This infrastructure allows the development of small villages, integrating them to the rest of the country and guaranteeing national sovereignty in the process. To support this process, there is in the platoon an element that contains representatives of the Federal Police, the Indian Foundation, the customs system and others.

Recently, the 3ʳᵈ Special Border Platoon, close to the Colombian frontier, was transformed into an independent company

MILITARY UNITS IN THE REGION

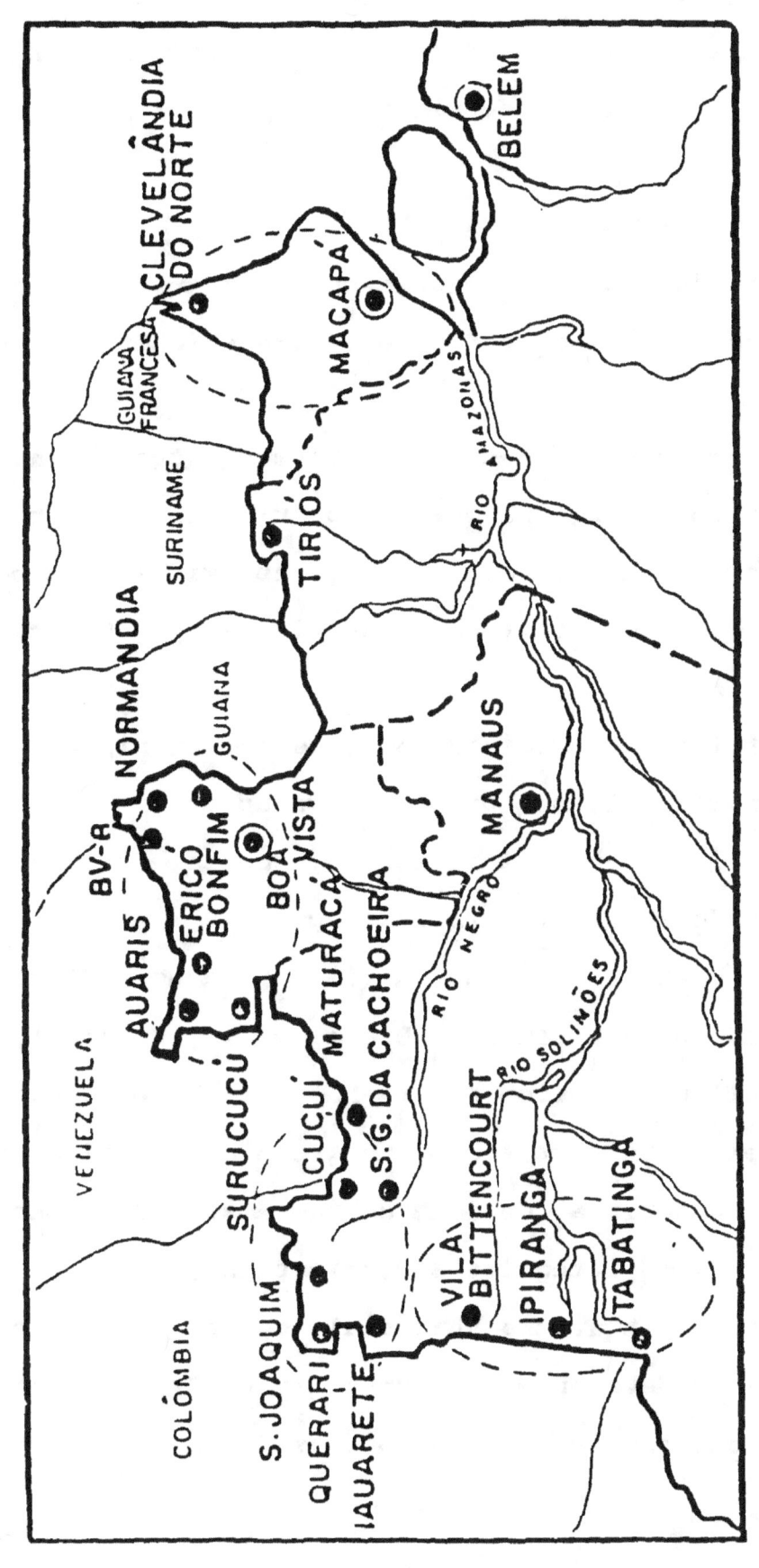

FIGURE 15

67

after the guerrilla raid made against that platoon by the Colombian Revolutionary Armed Forces (FARC) - Simón Bolivar Command - in Brazilian territory.

A PROPOSED STRATEGY

Strategies for Amazonian security must take into account the facts cited earlier in this paper, and which threaten national sovereignty.

As used in this thesis, the term _strategy_ means the art of developing and using the _means_ (power) available in the international context, considering the existing or potential _obstacles_, in order to reach specified _ends_ (objectives) of national policy.

The following premises underlie the thesis of this paper:

o Brazil will not want to give up power over the Amazon,

o in international relations, special interests predominate over friendship,

o if Brazil is denied the immediate use of its huge Amazonian potential, Brazil will, in effect, be denied full utilization of its National Power and, consequently delay its entry into the group of the first-world, and

o international designs on the Amazon run counter to Brazil's integrity and sovereignty.

To avoid situations that could compromise its sovereignty, or retard the development of the Amazon, Brazil must develop strategic actions in that region, as follows:

In the POLITICAL FIELD:

- to stimulate the developed countries into a more active participation in the area, <u>in a manner consistent with Brazil's national objectives</u>, through economic and technological support for an orderly development of that Amazon basin,

- to stem environmental depredation through measures aimed at surveillance of the region, and to provide human and material means to the interested agencies,

- to intensify diplomatic actions with governments of the developed countries, in particular those which have been applying the greatest pressure, in order to get funds, weaken that pressure, obtain technology, and neutralize the interference of specific international organizations in the area,

- to intensify integration of the Amazonian countries through strengthening of the Amazon Pact; other countries must be brought to believe that Brazil does not aspire to regional hegemony,

- to re-equip the Brazilian Federal Police so that it may better accomplish its missions, particularly those related to combatting narcotics trafficking,

- to analyze the possibility of politically reorganizing the area, to better identify needs and allocate and administer resources,

- to strengthen existing projects, such as Calha Norte and Our Nature[85],

- to seek a diplomatic understanding with Venezuela on common issues related to the Yanomami indigenous community and Brazilian gold miners, and

- to shift from a defensive posture on the international scene to a proactive one in order to neutralize any interventionism campaign and to show Brazil's capability to solve and manage the area's problems.

In the ECONOMIC FIELD:

- To develop economic programs, mainly in civil construction and shipbuilding, that develop the region by taking advantage of the area's favorable conditions for growing timber,

- to reform national financial and economic structures so as to make them capable of addressing the needs of the Amazonian region,

- to exploit hydroelectric potential, strengthening the main centers and contributing to the policy of integrating the region into the National center,

- to equip the ports of the huge waterway system, remove the obstacles to river navigation, build locks where the projects may require them, strengthen the existing highways, and build railroads where practicable, thus making it possible for people and resources to circulate and making possible a greater economic and social integration of the area,

- to classify forest areas for economic and social activities, environmental preservation, and allocation to indigenous communities,

- to support and coordinate responsible actions by environmental organizations,

- to construct roads and railways improving access to the Caribbean via Caracas and/or Georgetown, and also to the Pacific via Peru and/or Chile, thus giving Brazil access to the maritime routes of those countries, reducing transport costs, and thereby increasing the export of Brazilian agricultural products,

- to support and coordinate the actions of teaching and research organizations towards development of "amazon" technology and definition of economic activities that improve the ecological balance,

- to establish reforestation rules for areas being exploited economically,

- to provide incentives for private enterprises to exploit economic resources without damaging the environment,

- to find international partners for social and economic development projects, preferably as "joint ventures", and

- to create and stimulate economic centers whose benefits would spread throughout the whole area.

In the SOCIOPSYCHOLOGICAL FIELD:

- to seek to motivate Brazilian society, when conditions for this are favorable, to overcome the obstacles arising from the region's backwardness,

- to reduce or eliminate narcotics trafficking,

- to inhibit or eliminate smuggling,

71

- to improve the capability of the Federal Police Department to deal with the above,

- to create in Brazilian society, and in particular in the Amazon region, an awareness of the role of the Armed Forces as an essential instrument to guarantee independence and national sovereignty,

- to avoid destruction of the ethical values of the indigenous communities, and oppose, by all means, any attempts at creating autonomous racial or ethnic enclaves in Brazilian territory, desired by international environmental and religious entities,

- to implement the indian policy in order to reduce the "indian against white" conflict fanned by the international media and by part of the clergy,

- to prevent the presence of foreigners who foment divisive actions among the indigenous communities, as well as assure more permanent presence of the Brazilian government's authorities, who are charged with listening more closely to the genuine interests and aspirations of the Yanomamis and other groups or indian communities,

- to promote campaigns for the enlightenment of national and international public opinion on the actions taken to solve the problems of the area, aiming to unmask the real intentions of those now using the ecological issue as an excuse to reach other less-noble objectives, and

- to give special attention to human resource development, particularly investing in education and training at all levels to promote the region's development and its integration into the rest of the country.

In the MILITARY FIELD:

- to support, if necessary, the fight against narcotics trafficking,

- to provide better support to the government's control and disciplinary actions in the area,

- to give special priorities to military communications facilities in forest areas. This action is currently near completion,

- to carry out the planned installation of military units in the area,

- to energize the Calha Norte project and support human settlement all along the frontiers of the region through an increase in military units, particularly in unpopulated spaces, as well as use and support of federal public servants and creating of public health infrastructure, basic sanitation, education, and housing,

- to carry out a public relations campaign to show all the world that the presence of Brazilian Armed Forces close to Brazil's borders demonstrates Brazil's strong will to preserve national sovereignty,

- to give priority to equipping, organizing, and training military units in the area, so they can deploy rapidly if necessary,

- to carry out field training exercises in the region to optimize the use of military power in case of need and to attenuate the activities of guerrilla groups in the region,

- to restudy the "Order of Battle", in order to increase the military presence in the area directed against narcotraffickers and guerrilla groups in the border zones,

- to set up and operate a Combined Operational Staff in the area, followed by the setting up of a Combined Military Area Command,

- to improve the 2nd Construction Engineering Group's capabilities to construct strategic roads in the area,

- to seek support in materiel, economic, and technological resources, -- but not the use of their Armed Forces -- from the developed countries to help solve the area's problems, and

- to maintain trained, highly mobile, light units within the Amazon able to deploy rapidly to any part of the region.

SUMMARY AND CONCLUSIONS

The line of reasoning in this paper intended to present:

o   what one wishes to secure - Area analysis

o   what and whom to secure from - The threat

o   how to secure - The prescription for the area's
security.

As has already been made clear, the nature of the threat to the security of the Amazon area is such that one cannot avoid focusing on the political and strategic level.

SUMMARY

The following thoughts will try to summarize this paper and reinforce its main ideas:

- the Brazilian people, as a natural and historical process, began to occupy the Amazon area and carry out its economic development,

- this development began in a very disorganized way,

- as the Amazon is one of the last unspoiled regions in the world, with immense, invaluable vegetable and mineral potential, future strategic decisions by the Brazilian people will inevitably affect their country's political and economic status,

- given a developed and economically integrated Amazon, Brazilian products will be able to successfully compete and secure a place in the world's markets,

- in consequence of the above, Brazil will grow stronger economically, and be able to improve the living standards of its population greatly,

- political, economic, and technological groups of the so-called "first world" feel their positions are threatened and proceed according to their historical interventionist tendency; There has been a movement to take advantage of the failures caused by the disorganized initial occupation and exploration of the area by using well-planned psychological methods beginning with a worldwide campaign to discredit Brazil at all levels of society,

- industrialized countries with limited availability of raw material, energy, and basic products that wish to strengthen their relations with Brazil come under economic and political pressure from other industrialized countries to prevent them from supporting the economic development of Brazil,

- ecological organizations, misled by manipulated information and half-truths typical of psychological actions, join in adding to the pressure on Brazil,

- several authorities with international status (including some heads of government, as cited early in this paper), either due to political interests (in most cases) or through ignorance, began to question Brazil's sovereignty over the area, thus raising a clear challenge to Brazilian sovereignty,

- the greater Brazilian military presence in the frontier region that the Calha Norte project entails will reduce illegal actions in the area, and prevent the uncontrolled outflow of natural resources. At the same time, it will bar the entry of guerrilla groups and drugtraffickers into Brazilian territory,

- the redefinition of the government's policy toward indigenous communities and the demarcation of their reserves will eliminate the sources of tension that threaten Brazilian security. This will thus protect the indigenous population and undercut the pretensions of international organizations that want to create politically autonomous "Indian Nations", which could be a danger to Brazil's integrity and sovereignty,

- no matter what the forms assumed by international special interest groups, the arguments those groups utilize are always non-preservation of the environment and the irrational use of the abundant natural resources of the area. Maintaining Brazil's sovereignty, therefore, depends on the integral and responsible settlement of the area,

- finally, world public opinion seems entirely inclined to support any initiatives towards "saving" the Amazon and, therefore, the planet;

- so, Brazilian sovereignty over the Amazonian area again becomes clearly threatened from another direction,

- thus it is appropriate to talk of the "security" of the Amazon, and

- security must be ensured through action in the political, economic, social and military fields.

CONCLUSIONS

o The occupation of the Amazon area is an absolutely legitimate right of the Brazilian people, encouraged and promoted by the recent Brazilian governments, that helps gain the nation's permanent aims of national integration, progress, and social peace,

o Despite the initial disorganization which led to several internal conflicts, this occupation is taking place and shall be conducted towards a successful ending in accordance with another fundamental national aim, democracy,

o The Brazilian rejection of foreign interference in their internal affairs is also legitimate and is supported by other national aims of national patrimony, integrity, and sovereignty,

o Even if the aim of the "Amazonian debate" is fair and just (to prevent the Amazon rain forest against ecological aggression), this is a Brazilian task and responsibility. Foreign "tutelage" and/or political impositions are unacceptable. Brazil cannot renounce its right to exploit the natural resources of the Amazon. The article 3 of the Brazilian Constitution states that: " the followings are objectives of the Brazilian Republic:

. to guarantee natural development and

. to eradicate poverty and ... reduce social and regional inequalities."

o The Brazilian nation is quite capable of finding solutions to its internal problems and applying them with the "help" of responsible foreign organizations,

o Given their peaceful and Christian character, the Brazilian people are capable of building their future and improving their welfare,

o But the Brazilian people will also be able to identify and will repel any attempts at interference with their sovereignty.

Finally, to achieve the security of the Brazilian Amazon area, the methods to be used are:

1 - increased military presence in the region,

2 - development of sustainable economic activities,[86]

3 - improved access to new environmentally-related technologies that preserve the ecosystem and the environment,

4 - the application of resources from the international financial institutions (e.g. the World Bank and the Inter American Development Bank), and

5 - collaboration in good faith of the industrialized countries.

Nothing can better reflect the Brazilian people's will, determination, and enthusiasm to secure and integrate the Amazon area than this phrase from a great soldier, General Rodrigo Otávio, engraved on the garrisons in the Amazon: *"Hard is the mission of defending and developing the Amazon, but harder was that of our ancestors in conquering and maintaining it."*

ENDNOTES

[1]Aderbal de Meira Mattos, "O Interesse Nacional e os Interesses Internacionais na Amazonia Brasileira", _Revista Brasileira de Estudos Políticos_, July 1990 (no.71), 105-106.

[2]Christian Church World Council, _Directive Brazil no 4_, Geneva - July 1991, 1-2.

[3]Orna Feldman, "Rain Forest Chic", _The New Republic_, 25 June 1990, 20.

[4]Gilberto Mestrinho, "Mestrinho identifica complô", _Correio Braziliense_ -Brasília-DF, 19 July 1991, 5.

[5]Tyler Bridges, "Will new Road in Amazon Pave Way for Wealth or Devastation", _The Christian Science Monitor_, 23 September 1988, 7.

[6]Euler Ribeiro," A Amazônia Intocada", _O Globo_ - Rio de Janeiro - 24 July 1991, 6.

[7]Reuters, "Brazil Denies Japan Deal", _The New York Times_, 06 February 1991, 5.

[8]Thaumaturgo Sotero Vaz, "Sotero Vaz comments on defense of Amazon", _Daily Report - Latin America_, 06 February 1992, 23.

Michael S. Serrill, "A Dubious Plan for the Amazon", _Time_, 17 April 1989, 67.

[9]Sharon Begley et al.,"The World's Largest Lab", _Newsweek_, 20 February 1989, 47.

[10]Eugene Linden, "Playing with Fire", _Time_, 18 September 1989, 32.

[11]Dick Thompson, "A Global Agenda for the Amazon", _Time_, 18 September 1989, 38.

[12]Cláudio Heráclito Souto, Manoel da Penha Alves, Julio Cesar Barbosa Hernandes, Paulo Roberto Correa Assis, Carlos Alberto Pinto Silva, "Ameaças à Soberania na Amazônia", A Defesa Nacional - Rio de Janeiro - volume 752 - April/June 1991, 26.

[13]John Heinz & Timothy Wirth, "What We Can Do To Save The Rainforests", _The Christian Science Monitor_, 16 February 1989, 18.

[14]William Booth, "Amazon Area Indians Wory Of The Rain Forest Plans", _The Washington Post_, 20 October 1989, A-4.

[15]Dick Thompson, 38.

[16]Oziel Carneiro, "Amazônia, hipoteca ecológica?", _Jornal do Brasil_ - Rio de Janeiro, 24 July 1991, 8.

[17]Patricia Saboia, "Tribunal dos Povos julga Brasil culpado por devastar a Amazônia", _O Globo_ - Rio de Janeiro, 17 October 1990, 19.

[18]Silvia Palacios, "Brazilians ready to fight Bush's new world order", EIR Feature - 6 September 1991, 17.

[19]Agência O Globo, "Anúncio anti-BIRD Destaca Rondonia", _O Globo_ - Rio de Janeiro, 17 October 1990, 19.

[20]Sotero Vaz, 23.

[21]Leônidas Pires Gonçalves, Exposição do Ministro do Exérctio ao Senado Federal, Brasília-DF, 04 April 91, 3.

[22]Leandro Tocantins, Euclides da Cunha e o Paraíso Perdido, (Gráfica e Editora Record - Rio de Janeiro - 1966), 8.

[23]Samuel Benchimol, O Desenvolvimento da Amazônia Brasileira, Palestra na Escola Superior de Guerra - Rio de Janeiro - 1989, 4.

[24]Editora Abril, Almanaque Abril 1991, Gráfica e Editora Abril - Rio de Janeiro - 1991, 109.

[25]Enjolras José Castro Camargo, Estudos de Problemas Brasileiros, (BIBLIEX - Rio de Janeiro - 1979), 127.

[26]Ibid, 131.

[27]Editora Abril, Almanaque Abril 1991, Gráfica e Editora Abril - Rio de Janeiro - 1991, 114.

[28]Ministério do Interior, Primeiro Plano de Desenvolvimento da Amazônia, Brasília -DF- 1986/1989, 35.

[29]Eugene Linden, 34-35.

[30]Ibid, 36.

[31]Herbert O. R. Schubart, Diagnosis of the Natural Resources of Amazonia, Brazil's National Institute for Research in Amazonia - Manaus - 31 August 1989, 3-4.

[32]Ibid, 4.

[33]Centro de Comunicação Social do Exército, "27 anos treinando soldados na Amazônia, O Verde-Oliva, Brasília -DF- 1991, 8.

[34]Ibid, 8-9.

[35]Capistrano de Abreu, Capítulos da História Colonial, Rio de Janeiro -1969, 29.

[36]The Treaty of Tordesilhas was signed between Portugal and Spain in 1494 and it dealt with both the discovered and to be discovered lands. The two kings agreed to draw an imaginary meridian 370 leagues (measure of distance: one league equal to

3.72 miles) westward of the Green Cape Islands. All the lands to the east of this line would belong to Portugal; the ones to the west to Spain.

[37]"Bandeirantes" was the name given to both the chief and the members of the expeditions to Brazil's inland. These expeditions were financed either by the king of Portugal or individuals, and they were responsibles by the enlargement of the early Brazil's borders from the sixteenth to the eighteen centuries, because many of them crossed the Tordesilhas Treaty's line. All the boundary disputes so created were resolved latter by means of new agreements: Lisbon Treaty (1681), "Utrech" (1713-1715), "Madrid" (1750), Santo Ildefonso (1777) and "Badajoz" (1801). Manoel M. Albuquerque, Arthur C.F. Reis, Carlos D. Carvalho, Atlas Histórico Escolar, Ministério da Educação e Cultura, Fundação Nacional de Material Escolar, Rio de Janeiro, 1980, 44.

[38]Artur César Ferreira Reis, A Amazônia e a Cobiça Internacional, Editora Civilização Brasileira - Rio de Janeiro -1982, 30.

[39]Uti-Possidetis- a principle of international law that a conclusion of treaty of peace between belligerents vests in them respectively as absolute property the territory under their actual control and the things attached to it and the movables then in their possession except as otherwise stipulated (as by treaty), The Webster's Third New International Dictionary, Springfield - MA - 1981, 2808

[40]E. Bradford Burns, The Unwritten Alliance: Rio Branco and Brazilian-American Relations, New York: Columbia University

Press, 1966, 44.

[41]Thomas G. Sanders, "Brazilian Geopolitics: Securiting the South and North", UFSI Reports, Universities Field Staff International ,Inc., Indianapolis, no.23/1987, 6.

[42]Terezinha de Castro, Geopolítica do Brasil, BIBLIEX _ Rio de Janeiro - 1986, 16.

[43]Romeu Tuma, "Há Problemas no Combate ao Tráfico de Drogas", Folha de São Paulo - 23 June 1991, 5.

[44]Constituição do Brasil, Artigo no 144 - Parágrafo 1, Brasília - DF - 03 October 1988, 70.

[45]Vera Lucia Canfran, "Armed Forces' Role in Antidrug Effort", Daily Report - Latin America, 26 September 1991, 21.

[46]Luiz Augusto de Araújo Castro, Narcotic Drugs, Statement at the U.N. Economic and Social Council - New York - 10 June 1991, 1.

[47]Editora Abril, Brasil dia a dia, Gráfica e Editora Abril - Rio de Janeiro - 1991, 234.

[48]Almanaque Abril 1991, 249.

[49]Michael Kidron and Ronald Segal, The New State of the World Atlas, New York, 1987, 48.

[50]Helena Salem, "Civilização virou Sinônimo de Desastre", Jornal do Brasil - Caderno de Ecologia -, Rio de Janeiro, 8 July 1991, 3.

[51]Armando Simões de Castro Filho, O Projeto Calha Norte e os Países limítrofes da Área. Brazilian National Defense College, Rio de Janeiro - RJ, 1990, 29.

[52]Christian Church World Council, 3.

[53]Brasil dia a dia, 23

[54]Ibid, 234.

[55]Cláudio, Manoel, Julio Cesar, Paulo Roberto, Carlos Alberto, 18.

[56]Linden, 33.

[57]Ibid, 34.

[58]Philip M. Fearnside, <u>Deforestation Rate in Brazilian Amazonia</u>, National Institute for Research in Amazonia - Manaus - August 1990, 2.

[59]Ibid,3.

[60]Philip Fernanside, "Desmatamento só diminui por causa da crise de Ecologia", <u>*Jornal do Brasil*</u> - Caderno de Ecologia - 12 August 1991, 3.

[61]Constituição do Brasil, <u>Artigo 23 - Parágrafo VII</u>, Brasília - DF - 3 October 1988, 23.

[62]Eurípedes Alcântara, "A ciência afasta o perigo do desastre global", <u>*VEJA*</u> - São Paulo - 9 October 1991, 83.

[63]Carlos de Meira Mattos, "La internacinalización de la Amazonia', <u>*GEOSUR*</u> Revista - no 113/114 - Sep/Oct 1989, 29.

[64]Ibid, 30.

[65]Ibid.

[66]Ibid, 31.

[67]Ibid, 32.

[68]Ibid.

[69]Aderbal de Meira Mattos, 104.

[70]Ibid, 105.

[71]Ibid.

[72]Ibid, 106.

[73]Araujo Castro, "Freeze the strucutre of World Power", <u>The Times</u>, 8 March 1989, 12. Josemar Dantas, "A teoria do Butim", *Correio Braziliense*, Brasília - DF, 23 June 1991, 4.

[74]The Brazilian National Defense College (Escola Superior de Guerra), in its basic manual entitled "Doutrina" (Doctrine), aims the Brazilian Permanent National Objectives as being: Democracy, National Integration, Integrity of National Patrimony, Social Peace, Progress and Sovereignty. Rio de Janeiro, 1989, 68.

[75]Amazonino Mendes, "Amazonas quer se desenvolver sem destruição", *O Globo* - Rio de Janeiro - 5 July 1991, 9.

[76]Almanaque Abril 1991, 181.

[77]Antonio Tebaldi Tardin and Luiz Gylvan Meira Filho, "<u>Greenhouse effect in Amazonia</u>, Brazil's Institute for Space Research, São Paulo, April 1991, 5.

[78]Ibid, 6

[79]Leônidas Pires Gonçalves, <u>Amazonas: Ecologia e Soberania</u>, Discurso no Superior Tribunal de Justiça - Brasília - DF - 23 August 1989, 21.

[80]Ibid, 23.

[81]Daily Report - Latin America, <u>Collor signs Decree creating Reservation</u>, *Rede Globo Television* - Rio de Janeiro - 15 November 1991, 46.

[82]Armando Castro Filho, 7.

[83]Thomas G. Sanders, 7.

[84]Evandro Bartholomei Vidal, <u>O Projeto Calha Norte - importância</u>

para a Região Amazônica e seus reflexos na Segurança Nacional,
(*ECEME* - Rio de Janeiro - 1991), 20.

[85]In April 1989, José Sarney Administration launched the *Nossa Natureza ("OUR NATURE")* program as a major response to external pressure. It was directed towards the reduction of predatory action against the environment and the renewable natural resources in the Brazilian Amazon, with emphasis placed on the creation of an emergency plan of control and fiscalization to combat deforestation and burnings in the region. Andrew Hurrell, "The Politics of Amazonian Deforestation", *Journal of Latin American Studies* - February - Volume 23 - no 1 - 1991, 207.

[86]Sustainable economic activities are those which exploit the natural resources of the region without harming the environment or depleting the resource.

BIBLIOGRAPHY

Abreu, Capistrano. <u>Capítulos da História Colonial</u>. Rio de
Janeiro, 1969: 29 and 38.

Albuquerque, Manoel M.; Reis, Arthur C.F.; Carvalho, Carlos
Delgado. <u>Atlas Histórico Escolar</u>. Ministério da Educação e
Cultura, Fundação Nacional do Material Escolar, Rio de
Janeiro, 1980: 44.

Alcântara, Eurípides. "A Ciência afasta o perigo do desastre
global". <u>VEJA</u> , São Paulo, 9 October 1991 : 81-91.

Benchimol, Samuel. <u>O Desenvolvimento da Amazônia Brasileira</u>.
Palestra na Escola Superior de Guerra, Rio de Janeiro, 1989.

Begley, Sharon et al. "The Wolrl's largest Lab". <u>Newsweek</u>, 20
February 1989: 47.

Berlineck, Deborah. "Efeito Estufa: Países-ilhas lideram debate".
<u>O Globo</u>, Rio de Janeiro, 13 July 1991: 23.

Booth, William. "Amazon Area Indians Wory Of Rain Forest Plans".
<u>The Washington Post</u>, 20 October 1989: A-4.

Bridges, Tyler. "Will New Road In Amazon Pave Way For Wealth Or
Devastation?". <u>The Christian Science Monitor</u>, 23 September
1988: 7.

Burns, E. Bradford. <u>The Unwritten Alliance: Rio Branco and
Brazilian-American Relations</u>. (New York: Columbia University
Press - 1966): 44.

Camargo, Enjolras José Castro. <u>Estudos de Problemas Brasileiros</u>.
BIBLIEX, Rio de Janeiro, 1979: 127-131.

Canfran, Vera Lucia. "Armed Forces' Role in Antidrug Effort

Discussed". <u>Daily Report - Latin America</u>, 26 September: 21.

Carneiro, Oziel. "Amazônia, hipoteca ecológica?". <u>Jornal do Brasil</u>, Rio de Janeiro, 24 July 1991: 8.

Castro, Araujo. "Freeze the Structure of World Power". <u>The Times</u>, 8 March 1989: 12.

Castro, Luiz Augusto de Araújo. <u>Narcotic Drugs</u>. Statement at the U.N. Economic and Social Council, New York, 10 June 1991.

Castro Filho, Armando Simões. <u>O Projeto Calha Norte e os Países limítrofes da Área</u>. Escola Superior de Guerra, Rio de Janeiro, 1990.

Castro, Terezinha de. <u>Geopolítica do Brasil</u>. BIBLIEX, Rio de Janeiro, 1986.

Centro de Comunicação Social do Exército. "27 anos treinando soldados na Amazônia". <u>O VERDE-OLIVA</u>, Brasília, DF, 1991: 8-9.

Christian Church World Council. <u>Directive Brazil no 4</u>. Geneva, July 1991: 1-3.

Constituição do Brasil. <u>Artigo no 23 - Parágrafo VII and Artigo 144 - Parágrafo I</u>. (Brasília, DF, 03 October 1988): 23 and 70.

Dantas, Josemar. "A Teoria do Butim". <u>Correio Braziliense</u>. Brasília-DF, 23 June 1991: 4.

Daily Report - Latin America. <u>Collor signs Decree creating reservation</u>. Rede Globo Television, Rio de Janeiro, 15 November 1991.

Editora Abril. <u>Almanaque Abril 1991</u>. Gráfica e Editora Abril. Rio de Janeiro, 1991: 109 and 114.

Editora Abril. <u>Brasil dia a dia</u>. Gráfica e Editora Abril, Rio de Janeiro, 1991: 234.

Ellis, William S. "Brazil's Imperiled Rain Forest". <u>National Geographic</u>. Washington, Volume 174, no 6, December 1986: 772-779.

Fearnside, Philip M. <u>Deforestation Rate in Brazilian Amazonia</u>. National Institute for Research in Amazonia. Manaus, AM August 1990.

Fearnside, Philip M. "Desmatamento só diminui por causa da crise de Ecologia". <u>Jornal do Brasil</u> - Caderno de Ecologia - Rio de Janeiro, 12 August 1991: 3.

Fearnside, Philip M. "Deforestation in Amazonia". <u>Environment</u>. (May 1989): 17-40.

Feldman, Orna. "Rain Forest Chic". <u>The New Republic</u>, 25 June 1990: 20.

Gonçalves, Leônidas Pires. <u>Amazonas: Ecologia e Soberania</u>. Discurso no Superior Tribunal de Justiça. Brasília, DF, 23 August 1989: 21 and 23.

Guerra, Escola Superior de. <u>Doutrina</u>. Rio de Janeiro, 1990.

Guimarães, Roberto. "Ecopolitica de la Amazonia". <u>GEOSUR</u>, Nov-Dec 1990, Volume 12, no 127-128: 16-22.

Heinz, John and Wirt, Timothy, "What We Can Do To Save The Rai Forests". <u>The Christian Science Monitor</u>, 16 February 1989: 18.

Hurrel, Andrew. "The Politics of Amazonian Deforestation" _Journal of Latin American Studies_. (February 1991, Volume 23, no 1).

Junior, Policarpo. "A Espera da Guerra". _VEJA_. São Paulo, 22 January 1992: 8.

Kidron, Michael; Segal, Ronald. _The New State of the World Atlas_. New York, 1987.

Linden, Eugene. "Playing with Fire". _Time_. New York, 18 September 1989: 33-34.

Martim, Alvim Marseno. _A Amazônia e Nós_. BIBLIEX, Rio de Janeiro, 1971.

Mattos, Aderbal de Meira. "O interesse Nacional e os interesses internacionais na Amazônia Brasileira". _Revista Brasileira de Estudos Políticos_. Rio de Janeiro, July 1990: 104-106.

Mattos, Carlos de Meira. "La internacionalizacíon de la Amazonia". _Geosur Revista_. (Sep/Oct 1989 - no 113/114): 30-32.

Mattos, Carlos de Meira. _Uma Geopolítica Pan-Amazônica_. BIBLIEX, Rio de Janeiro, 1980.

Mercado Jarrin, Edgardo. "Seguridad y Ecologia. Reformulacíon de un concepto". _Nueva Sociedad_. (May/June 1990 - no 107): 21-26.

McIntyre, Loren. "Last Days of Eden". _National Geographic_. Washington, Volume 174, no 6, December 1988: 800-817.

Ministério do Interior. _Primeiro Plano de Desenvolvimento da Amazônia_. (Brasília, DF, 1986/1989).

Mendes, Amazonino. "Amazonas quer se desenvolver sem destruição".
O Globo, Rio de Janeiro, 5 July 1991.

Mestrinho, Gilberto. "Mestrinho indentifica complô". Correio
Braziliense, Brasília-DF, 19 July 1991: 5.

Palacios,Silvia. "Brazilians ready to fight Bush's new world
order". EIR Feature. (6 September 1991).

Poppins, Rollie E. Brazil - The Land and People. New York, Oxford
University Press, 1968.

Raben, Linda. "Brazil's Military Stakes its Claim". The Nation,
12 March 1990: 341-342.

Reis, Artur César Ferreira. A Amazônia e a Cobiça Internacional.
Editora Civilização Brasileira, Rio de Janeiro, 1982.

Reuters Agency. "Brazil Denies Japan Deal". The New York Times, 6
February 1991, 5.

Ribeiro, Euler. "A Amazônia Intocada". O GLOBO, Rio de Janeiro,
24 July 1991: 6.

Rodrigues, Danubio; Monteiro, Joaquim. "Militares vão ocupar a
Amazônia". Correio Braziliense. Brasília, DF, 23 July 1991:
8.

Saboia, Patricia. "Tribunal dos Povos julga Brasil culpado por
devastar a Amazonia". O Globo, 17 October 1990: 19.

Sanders, Thomas G. "Brazilian Geopolitcs: Securing the South and
North". UFSI Reports, Universities Field Staff, Inc.,
Indianapolis, 1987/No.23: 7.

Salem, Helena. "Civilização significa desastre". Jornal do Brasil
- Caderno de Ecologia - Rio de Janeiro, 8 July 1991: 3.

Schubart, Herbert O. R. <u>Diagnosis of the Natural Resources of</u>
<u>Amazonia</u>. Brazil's National Institute for Research in
Amazonia, Mamaus, 31 August 1989.

Seixas, Mário de Oliveira. "Defence of the Amazon Area". <u>Royal</u>
<u>Staff College</u>. England, 1989.

Serril, Michael S. "A Dubious Plan for the Amazon". <u>Time</u>, 17
April 1989: 23.

Smith, Nigel; Plucknett, Williams; Plucknett, Donald. "Conserving
the Tropical Cornucopia". <u>Environment</u> (July - August   1991-
volume 33, no 6): 6-9, 30-32.

Souto, Claudio Heráclito; Alves, Manoel da Penha; Hernandes,
Julio Cesar Barbosa; Assis, Paulo Roberto Correa; Pinto
Silva, Carlos Alberto. "Ameaças à Soberania na Amazônia". <u>A</u>
<u>Defesa Nacional</u>, Rio de Janeiro, Volume 752, April/June
1991: 17-18, 29-32.

Tardim, Antônio Tebaldi; Meira Filho, Luiz Gylvan. "Greenhouse
effect in Amazonia". <u>Brazil's Institute for Space Research</u>.
São Paulo, April 1991: 5-6.

Thompson, Dick. "A Global Agenda for the Amazon." <u>Time</u>, 18
September: 38.

Tocantins, Leandro. <u>Euclides da Cunha e o Paraíso Perdido</u>.
Gráfica e Editora Record, Rio de Janeiro, 1966.

Tuma, Romeu. "Há Problemas no Combate ao Tráafico de Drogas".
<u>Folha de São Paulo</u>, 23 June 1991: 5.

Valente, Maury Gurgel; Coimbra, Carlos; Albuquerque Lima, Afonso Augusto; et al. _Problemática da Amazônia_. BIBLIEX, Rio de Janeiro, 1971.

Vaz, Thaumaturgo Sotero. "Sotero Vaz comments on Defense of Amazon". _Daily Report-Latin America_, 6 February 1992, 23.

Vidal, Evandro Bartholomei. _O Projeto Calha Norte - importancia para a Região Amazônica e seus reflexos na Segurança Nacional_. ECEME, Rio de Janeiro, 1991.

Webster's Third New International Dictionary. _Uti-Possidetis_. (Springfield, MA, 1981): 280

www.ingramcontent.com/pod-product-compliance
Lightning Source LLC
Chambersburg PA
CBHW081226280526
45787CB00006B/2546